KNITTING OFF

PROJECTS + TECHNIQUES FOR SIDEWAYS KNITTING

THE *axis*

MATHEW GNAGY

INTERWEAVE.
interweave.com

EDITOR   Ann Budd
TECHNICAL EDITOR   Lori Gayle
ART DIRECTOR   Liz Quan
DESIGN   Julia Boyles
PHOTOGRAPHY   Joe Hancock
PHOTO STYLING   Carol Beaver
HAIR AND MAKEUP   Jessica Shinyeda
ILLUSTRATIONS   Gayle Ford
PRODUCTION   Katherine Jackson

Interweave Press LLC
201 East Fourth Street
Loveland, CO 80537-5655 USA
Interweave.com

Printed in China by Asia Pacific Offset Ltd.

Library of Congress
Cataloging-in-Publication Data

Gnagy, Mathew.
Knitting off the axis : projects
& techniques for sideways
knitting / Mathew Gnagy.
    p. cm.
  Includes index.
  ISBN 978-1-59668-311-2 (pbk)
  ISBN 978-1-59668-887-2 (eBook)
1. Knitting--Patterns.
2. Knitting--Technique. I. Title.
  TT820.G593 2011
  746.43'2--dc23

2011012154

10 9 8 7 6 5 4 3 2 1

IN GRATITUDE

I would like to thank the following people, without whom this book would not have been possible.

Above all, I would like to thank Interweave for going out on a limb and accepting my book proposal. My editor, Ann Budd, deserves a huge heap of thanks! Also thank you to Lisa Shroyer of *Knitscene* magazine, who published my very first sweater pattern.

Thank you Ravi, Ruth, Jenn, Judi, Mark, Norma, Caroline, Nancy, Jens, Steven, Joyce, Jean, Emily, Leslie, and Carol. These people have been idea bouncers, pattern checkers, sample makers, knitting gurus, and moms. Extra special thanks to my "gang," Carlos, Randall, Don, Andrew, Erick, and Paul, who are always there with encouragement and love. Thank you to Alyssa, Lisa, Diana, and Pearl, as well as to shop owners, yarn store managers, editors, and more. And, of course, without the amazing technical editing by Lori Gayle, the patterns in this book might never have seen the light of day. I am quite sure that many more names should be in this list so thank you to everyone.

With much love, never-ending gratitude, and happy knitting,

Mathew Gnagy

CONTENTS

In earlier days, sideways knitting was usually confined to a dolman-style garment or a shapeless T. I have never subscribed to such one-dimensional thinking. Instead, I like to create nicely shaped underarms that will fit well

INTRODUCTION

against the body. In garments that do have a dolman styling, I have updated the look. In other cases, I have done away with traditional sweater shaping altogether and gone with geometric styles that seem prevalent in today's fashions.

I like to knit sideways because there are interesting variations on shapes that are easier to create with sideways knitting. With the use of cables, it is easier to use a cable panel as a hem rather than knitting it first and then picking up or sewing it on later. That said, several of the patterns in this book combine both horizontal and vertical cable panels, which makes it necessary to pick up stitches or apply a cable at the end of the knitting to achieve the desired effect.

To facilitate great shaping, I have tinkered with commonly accepted modes of shaping. For example, many sleeve increases are made in the interior of the sleeve, either centered over a couple of stitches or on each side of a central cable motif. These central increases force the active knitting edge into a curve, which results in a better fit and more streamlined finishing.

You will notice that there are many places where I ask you to bind off, only to pick up stitches on your bound-off edge later on in the work. Though it is possible to leave the stitches live until they're needed again, I would advise against it. Sideways knitting aligns the greater stretch of the fabric vertically along the body when worn. Gravity and wear will lengthen the garment.

By binding off the edge stitches and then picking up through them, you will create a much firmer edge that has less tendency to stretch out of shape over time.

Read through the techniques that follow and pay special attention if you decide to modify any of the patterns in this book. If a technique seems odd or deviates from traditional knitting, I suggest you just go with it—I have given much thought to when and where each technique is used to prevent the sideways knits from stretching in unexpected ways.

STITCH AND ROW GAUGE

In sideways knitting, gauge plays a much more vital role than in standard bottom-to-top construction. Whereas stitch gauge is of primary importance and row gauge can be largely ignored in most vertical knits, the opposite it true for sideways knits. When knitting sideways, you can fudge stitch gauge a bit toward the small side as gravity will stretch the garment somewhat within a couple of wearings. You cannot fudge row gauge.

For sideways knitting, you must knit a generous swatch that is at least 30 stitches wide and 40 rows long. Knit the swatch with the needles you plan to use and in the various stitch patterns specified in the instructions. Measure the number of stitches and rows, including fractions of stitches and rows, in 4" (10 cm) and divide by 4 to get the number of stitches and rows per inch (2.5 cm) of knitting. Keep in mind that the success of your garment depends on accurate gauge measurements. Don't hesitate to change needle size if necessary to obtain the correct gauge. The size needle you use is immaterial if you get the correct gauge.

WEAVING IN ENDS

I recommend that the tail ends of yarn are woven in before blocking or assembly occurs. This helps keep the work tidy and prevents the tails from being used to sew a seam. If a tail is used to sew a seam, it puts undue stress on the last stitch of the knitting. In extreme cases, the last stitch can break and the knitting can ravel. Weave in the ends as you complete each piece of a garment so there won't be so many when the knitting is completed.

MEASURING YOUR WORK

Accurate measurement of the knitting in progress is paramount for successful results. Never stretch the piece as you are measuring and always measure on a large flat surface such as a table or floor. Do not be tempted to measure on your leg, knitting bag, or arm of a chair. If you're like me and knit on the road (not while you're driving, please), apologize to your travel companions, stop the car, get out, and use the hood of the car as flat surface (note that this is less effective in rain or snow).

INTERNAL INCREASES AND DECREASES

Internal Increases are one of the most important features of my work. Applying these intelligently can create more developed shaping with a minimum of effort. For example, when knitting a sleeve, it is customary to put all increases at the edges of the work, most often one or two stitches in from the edge (where the seam will be). When placed more centrally on the sleeve, in contrast, they force the outer edges to align with the straight grain of the fabric. This causes the center of the sleeve to be slightly longer than the edges, which creates great shape for sleeve caps, particularly in drop-shoulder styles.

In general, internal increases can be worked on each side of a central stitch. For even better sleeve cap shaping, I prefer to separate the increases with a central panel of stitches. Most often this panel includes a cable pattern, but sometimes it is a simple band of 2" to 3" (5 to 7.5 cm) of stockinette.

When a piece of knitting needs to be made narrower, internal decreases have the same effect. (This is the technique commonly used to shape the crown of a hat.)

When combined with short-rows, internal increases and decreases become part of a powerful shaping system that allows creative knitters to spread their wings and soar. The possibilities are quite astounding. For most of the garments in *Knitting Off the Axis,* I kept the systems fairly simple. However, the three garments in Every Which Way, beginning on page 110, offer a glimpse of just how varied the applications can be.

CABLES

I use a lot of cables in my work—they create beautiful and interesting fabrics, they come in all shapes and sizes, and they can double as a means to shape a garment. For example, the natural take-up in width where the stitches in a cable cross can be used to draw in a waist or stabilize a shoulder.

Traditionally, cables are isolated in columns that look lovely but rarely interact with one another. I like the visual excitement of interacting cables. But keep in mind that traveling cables can affect gauge. You want to be sure to knit a gauge swatch that includes the entire traveling cable motif—more stitches will be required to knit an inch (2.5 cm) of cabled fabric than an inch (2.5 cm) of plain stockinette.

Quite often, left-leaning cables don't look as nice as right-leaning ones. It seems that the leftmost stitch tends to stretch disproportionately in a left-leaning cable. Careful attention to tension is required when working these cables to prevent this stretching. I find that I can conquer this problem if I work the final two stitches of the cable without removing these stitches from the left needle until both stitches have been worked.

The fast execution of well-balanced cables is mark of excellence for knitters. With a little practice, most of the cables in this book can be worked without a cable needle. This speeds up the knitting by minimizing excess handling of the stitches and juggling additional tools. See the Glossary for how to work cables without a cable needle.

When crossing a cable, the stitches on the back leg of the cross are hidden behind the front leg. If increases (or decreases) are worked in these hidden stitches, the increases (or decreases) become invisible. This is especially useful in patterns where a cable grows in size.

ASSEMBLY WITH CROCHET

Careful assembly of the pieces is as important to the overall success of a garment as the knitting. I usually join the pieces of my sideways garments with a crochet stitch (see Glossary), which is the preferred method in the sweater industry. It forms a strong and moderately elastic seam. In sideways knits, crocheted vertical seams have less of a tendency to stretch out of shape over time and, despite the slightly bulkier appearance, they have a professional look. To minimize bulk, work the join very close to the edge of each piece.

If you choose to use a mattress stitch or other sewn assembly method, work a double stitch every couple of inches (5 cm) to prevent the entire seam from opening should there be a break in the joining yarn.

BLOCKING AND PRESSING

To block or not to block—this is a great debate among knitters. Blocking helps even out the stitches, but it can also alter the finished size of a garment. The measurements are taken as a garment is knitted in its unblocked state; using a blocking method that changes those dimensions is counterproductive. Therefore, I rarely recommend blocking by submerging a garment in water, then stretching and pinning it to shape. This method puts undue stress on yarn and, without careful attention, a heavy, water-soaked sweater can stretch hopelessly out of shape.

I prefer to block with a quality steam iron and a pressing cloth (to protect the knitting from the hot iron). I generally use a damp pressing cloth and set the iron on the cloth for a second or two. This helps the stitches gently "fold" into one another and effectively "locks" them in place. Do not slide the iron across the cloth—this could cause the stitches to distort. In most cases, a bit of steam is all that's needed to even out the stitches and uncurl the edges. I only recommend submersion and stretching to shape if, and only if, your garment happens to end up a bit too small.

TRULY SIDEWAYS

My inspiration for the form and shape of my sweaters most often comes from the fashion metropolis of New York City. Frequently, as I walk about during my daily routine, I notice people wearing unique and unusual clothing. Tailored coats always intrigue me. Their stunning silhouettes help me discover compelling shapes that lend themselves beautifully to sideways construction.

Translating a shape from a woven to a knitted fabric often leads sweater designers to omit subtle shaping details that are generally too complicated for the average knitter or too lengthy for written instructions when created in traditional top-down (vertical) construction. When worked sideways, however, these details are easily achieved through strategic increases and decreases to produce horizontal darts and shaped hems.

Each design in this chapter is knitted entirely sideways (with the exception of some edgings and collars).

Cecilia (page 12) is unique in the unusual way the sleeve begins on the bias. It reflects one of my favorite aspects of knitting—shaping can take place anywhere in the fabric.

Becca (page 20) and Deille (page 30) retain much of the look of garments I saw on the streets of New York. Both cardigans feature bell sleeves and prominent collars, but a drop-shoulder gives Becca a more casual look than the tailored drape of Deille.

Francesca (page 42) grew into her own look after many unsuccessful permutations—I literally woke up one morning and the design had shifted in my mind to become the adorable quick-knit top that you see here. Loosely based on Francesca's silhouette, Talia (page 52) is a pullover with boatneck shaping. The perfect symmetry of the garment makes it an easy and satisfying knit. Similarly, the front and back are identical in Dani (page 58), but bust darts give this lightweight top a shape-enhancing fit.

The traditional and almost vintage look of Lynette (page 66) stands apart from the other garments in this chapter. But it is refreshed with interesting details, such as goblet cuffs and a fabulous collar.

For this textured pullover, I challenged myself to create a classic sideways sweater without the typical right-angle "T" shape. At the time, I was swatching for a garment knitted as a bias square. I combined the two ideas and Cecilia was born. The body begins with just a handful of stitches at the sleeve, then increases are worked at each end of the needle every right-side row. Talk about instant gratification—you'll be halfway across a body panel before you know it!

CECILIA

FINISHED SIZE

38½ (41½, 43, 47, 48½)" (98 [105.5, 109, 119.5, 123] cm) bust circumference.

Sweater shown measures 38½" (98 cm).

YARN

Worsted weight (#4 Medium).

Shown here: Cascade Yarns CashVero (55% merino, 33% microfiber, 12% cashmere; 125 yd [114 m]/50 g): #031 olive, 15 (17, 18, 21, 23) skeins.

NEEDLES

Size U.S. 7 (4.5 mm).

Adjust needle size if necessary to obtain the correct gauge.

NOTIONS

Cable needle (cn); stitch markers (m); removable markers or waste yarn; stitch holders; tapestry needle.

GAUGE

19 sts and 30½ rows = 4" (10 cm) in seed ridge patt.

12 sts of cable patt measure 2" (5 cm) wide.

stitch guide

2/2 RC: Sl 2 sts onto cable needle (cn) and hold in back, k2, k2 from cn.

2/2 RPC: Sl 2 sts onto cn and hold in back, k2, p2 from cn.

2/2 LPC: Sl 2 sts onto cn and hold in front, p2, k2 from cn.

CABLE (WORKED OVER 12 STS)

Row 1: (RS) P4, 2/2 RC, p4.

Row 2: (WS) K4, p4, k4.

Row 3: P2, 2/2 RPC, 2/2 LPC, p2.

Row 4: K2, p2, k4, p2, k2.

Row 5: P2, 2/2 LPC, 2/2 RPC, p2.

Row 6: K4, p4, k4.

Rep Rows 1–6 for pattern.

SEED RIDGE (ODD NUMBER OF STS)

Rows 1 and 3: (RS) Knit.

Rows 2 and 4: (WS) Purl.

Rows 5 and 6: K1, *p1, k1; rep from *.

Rep Rows 1–6 for pattern.

notes

+ The back and front are both worked sideways, beginning at one sleeve opening and ending at the other.

+ The collar and deep ribbed cuffs are worked separately and sewn to the body during finishing; these pieces are not shown on the schematic.

FRONT

Right Sleeve

CO 15 sts.

SET-UP ROW: (WS) K4, p4, k4, place marker (pm), p3.

Shape Lower Sleeve

ROW 1: (RS) K1f&b (see Glossary), knit to 2 sts before m (on first patt rep this will be 0 sts), k1f&b, k1, slip marker (sl m), work Row 1 of cable patt (see Stitch Guide) over 12 sts—2 sts inc'd.

ROW 2: Work Row 2 of cable patt, sl m, purl to end.

ROW 3: K1f&b, knit to 2 sts before m, k1f&b, k1, sl m, work Row 3 of cable patt—2 sts inc'd.

ROW 4: Work Row 4 of cable patt, sl m, purl to end.

ROW 5: K1f&b, *k1, p1; rep from * to 2 sts before m, k1f&b, k1, sl m, work Row 5 of cable patt—2 sts inc'd.

ROW 6: Work Row 6 of cable patt, sl m, k1, *p1, k1; rep from *.

Rep these 6 rows 3 (4, 5, 5, 6) more times—39 (45, 51, 51, 57) sts; piece measures 3¼ (4, 4¾, 4¾, 5¾)" (8.5 [10, 12, 12, 14.5] cm) from CO measured straight up along a single column of sts (do not measure along diagonal shaping).

NOTE: The underarm selvedge (beg of RS rows, end of WS rows) plus the CO edge will form the edge of the sleeve opening.

With RS facing, use a removable marker or waste yarn to mark beg of the last row completed to indicate where the sleeve seam should end.

Working even at underarm edge, cont to inc next to cable panel for shoulder as foll:

ROW 1: (RS) Knit to 2 sts before m, k1f&b, k1, sl m, work Row 1 of cable patt—1 st inc'd.

ROW 2: Work Row 2 of cable patt, sl m, purl to end.

ROW 3: Knit to 2 sts before m, k1f&b, k1, sl m, work Row 3 of cable patt—1 st inc'd.

ROW 4: Work Row 4 of cable patt, sl m, purl to end.

ROW 5: *K1, p1; rep from * to 3 sts before m, k1, k1f&b, k1, sl m, work Row 5 of cable patt—1 st inc'd.

ROW 6: Work Row 6 of cable patt, sl m, k2, *p1, k1; rep from *.

ROWS 7–10: Rep Rows 1–4 once.

ROW 11: *K1, p1; rep from * to 2 sts before m, k1f&b, k1, sl m, work Row 5 of cable patt—1 st inc'd.

ROW 12: Work Row 6 of cable patt, sl m, k1, *p1, k1; rep from *.

Rep the last 12 rows 1 (1, 1, 2, 2) more time(s), then work Rows 1–8 once more, ending with Row 2 of cable patt—55 (61, 67, 73, 79) sts; piece measures 7½ (8¼, 9, 10½, 11½)" (19 [21, 23, 26.5, 29] cm) from CO, measured straight up along a single column of sts, and 4¼ (4¼, 4¼, 5¾, 5¾)" (11 [11, 11, 14.5, 14.5] cm) from marked row along underarm selvedge.

Shape Underarm

Work even at shoulder while dec for underarm as foll:

ROW 1: (RS) BO 9 sts, knit to m, sl m, work Row 3 of cable patt—46 (52, 58, 64, 70) sts rem.

ROW 2: (WS) Work Row 4 of cable patt, sl m, purl to end.

ROW 3: K2tog, *p1, k1; rep from * to m, sl m, work Row 5 of cable patt—1 st dec'd.

ROW 4: Work Row 6 of cable patt, sl m, *k1, p1; rep from * to last st, k1.

ROW 5: K2tog, knit to m, sl m, work Row 1 of cable patt—44 (50, 56, 62, 68) sts rem.

ROW 6: Work Row 2 of cable patt, sl m, purl to end—piece measures 8¼ (9, 9¾, 11¼, 12¼)" (21 [23, 25, 28.5, 31] cm) from CO, measured straight up a single column of sts.

Place sts on holder, keeping m in position.

Right Side

CO 70 sts for all sizes.

SET-UP ROW: (WS) Purl to last 12 sts, pm, k4, p4, k4.

ROW 1: (RS) Work Row 1 of cable patt over 12 sts, sl m, knit to end.

ROW 2: (WS) Purl to m, sl m, work Row 2 of cable patt.

ROW 3: Work Row 3 of cable patt, sl m, knit to end.

ROW 4: Purl to m, sl m, work Row 4 of cable patt.

ROW 5: Work Row 5 of cable patt, sl m, *k1, p1; rep from * to end.

ROW 6: *P1, k1; rep from * to m, sl m, work Row 6 of cable patt.

ROW 7: Work Row 1 of cable patt, sl m, knit to end.

ROW 8: Purl to m, sl m, work Row 2 of cable patt.

ROW 9: Work Row 3 of cable patt, sl m, knit to last 2 sts, k1f&b, k1—71 sts.

ROW 10: Purl to m, sl m, work Row 4 of cable patt.

ROW 11: Work Row 5 of cable patt, sl m, *k1, p1; rep from * to last 3 sts, k1, k1f&b, k1—72 sts.

ROW 12: K2; *p1, k1; rep from * to m, sl m, work Row 6 of cable patt.

ROW 13: Work Row 1 of cable patt, sl m, knit to last 2 sts, k1f&b, k1—73 sts.

ROW 14: Purl to m, sl m, work Row 2 of cable patt—piece measures about 1¾" (4.5 cm) from CO.

Right Shoulder

JOINING ROW: (RS) Work Row 3 of cable patt over first 12 sts, sl m, knit to end, return 44 (50, 56, 62, 68) held sleeve sts to needle with RS facing and, keeping m in position, knit across sleeve sts to m, sl m, work Row 3 of cable patt over last 12 sts—117 (123, 129, 135, 141) sts total; 12 cable sts at each side; 93 (99, 105, 111, 117) center sts in seed ridge patt.

Mark this row (shown as dotted line on schematic) to indicate start of shoulder.

Beg with Row 4 of both patts, work even in patt for 34 (40, 40, 46, 46) rows, ending with RS Row 1 of patts—right shoulder measures 4½ (5¼, 5¼, 6¼, 6¼)" (11.5 [13.5, 13.5, 16, 16] cm) from marked shoulder row and piece measures 6¼ (7, 7, 8, 8)" (16 [18, 18, 20.5,

20.5] cm) from sts CO at right side.

Shape Front Neck

NEXT ROW: (WS) BO 14 sts, work in patt to m, sl m, work Row 2 of cable patt—103 (109, 115, 121, 127) sts rem.

NEXT 15 ROWS: Cont in patts, dec 1 st at neck edge (end of RS rows) on the next 8 RS rows by working last 3 sts as k2tog, k1, ending with RS Row 5 of patts—95 (101, 107, 113, 119) sts rem; 12 cable sts at lower edge, 83 (89, 95, 101, 107) seed ridge sts.

NEXT 19 (19, 25, 25, 31) ROWS: Work even, ending with WS Row 6 of patts.

NEXT 15 ROWS: Cont in patts, inc 1 st at neck on the next 8 RS rows by working to last st, M1 (see Glossary), k1, working new sts into established seed ridge patt and ending with RS Row 3 of patts—103 (109, 115, 121, 127) sts.

NEXT ROW: (WS) Use the cable method (see Glossary) to CO 14 sts, work Row 4 of cable patt over first 12 new sts, pm, purl to next m, sl m, work Row 4 of cable patt—117 (123, 129, 135, 141) sts; piece measures 6¾ (6¾, 7½, 7½, 8¼)" (17 [17, 19, 19, 21] cm) from sts BO at start of neck shaping.

Left Shoulder

Work even in patts for 35 (41, 41, 47, 47) rows, ending with RS Row 3 of patts—left shoulder measures 4½ (5¼, 5¼, 6¼, 6¼)" (11.5 [13.5, 13.5, 16, 16] cm) from sts CO at end of neck shaping.

Mark this row (shown as dotted line on schematic) to indicate end of left shoulder.

Break yarn and place last 44 (50, 56, 62, 68) sts just worked on holder for left sleeve, keeping m in position—73 lower body sts rem for all sizes.

Left Side

NEXT 7 ROWS: Cont in patts, dec 1 st at underarm (end of RS rows) on the next 3 RS rows by working last 3 sts as k2tog, k1, ending with Row 4 of patts—70 sts rem.

NEXT 7 ROWS: Work 6 rows even in patt, ending with WS Row 4 of patt, then knit 1 RS row—piece measures 1¾" (4.5 cm) from end of left shoulder and 19¼ (20¾, 21½, 23½, 24¼)" (49 [52.5, 54.5, 59.5, 61.5] cm) from sts CO for right side at start of body.

BO all sts.

Left Sleeve

Return 44 (50, 56, 62, 68) held sleeve sts to needles and rejoin yarn with WS facing.

Shape Underarm

NEXT 5 ROWS: Beg with WS Row 4 and cont in patts, inc 1 st at underarm (beg of RS rows) on next 2 RS rows by working first st as k1f&b, working new sts into seed ridge patt; end with WS Row 2 of patts—46 (52, 58, 64, 70) sts.

NEXT ROW: (RS) Use the cable method to CO 9 sts, work across new sts in established seed ridge patt from Row 3, sl m, work Row 3 of cable patt—55 (61, 67, 73, 79) sts; sleeve measures ¾" (2 cm) from end of left shoulder.

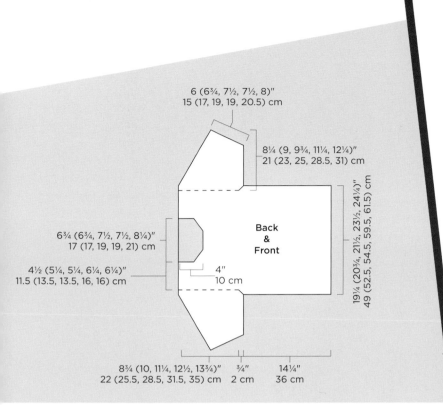

6 (6¾, 7½, 7½, 8)"
15 (17, 19, 19, 20.5) cm

8¼ (9, 9¾, 11¼, 12¼)"
21 (23, 25, 28.5, 31) cm

6¾ (6¾, 7½, 7½, 8¼)"
17 (17, 19, 19, 21) cm

4½ (5¼, 5¼, 6¼, 6¼)"
11.5 (13.5, 13.5, 16, 16) cm

Back & Front

4"
10 cm

19¼ (20¾, 21½, 23½, 24¼)"
49 (52.5, 54.5, 59.5, 61.5) cm

8¾ (10, 11¼, 12½, 13¾)"
22 (25.5, 28.5, 31.5, 35) cm

¾"
2 cm

14¼"
36 cm

Shape Lower Sleeve

NEXT 12 ROWS: Cont in patts, dec 1 st next to cable panel on the next 6 RS rows by working 3 sts before cable m as k2tog, k1; end with RS Row 3 of patts—49 (55, 61, 67, 73) sts rem.

Rep the last 12 rows 1 (1, 1, 2, 2) more time(s), then work the first 8 of the last 12 rows once more, ending with RS Row 5 of patts—39 (45, 51, 51, 57) sts rem; sleeve measures about 5 (5, 5, 6½, 6½)" (12.5 [12.5, 12.5, 16.5, 16.5] cm) from end of left shoulder.

With RS facing, use a removable marker or waste yarn to mark beg of the last row completed to indicate where the sleeve seam should end.

NEXT 6 ROWS: Cont in patts, dec 1 st at beg of row and dec 1 st next to cable

panel on the next 3 RS rows by working first 2 sts of row as ssk, and 3 sts before cable m as k2tog, k1; end with RS Row 5 of patts—33 (39, 45, 45, 51) sts rem.

NEXT 18 (24, 30, 30, 36) ROWS: Rep the last 6 rows 3 (4, 5, 5, 6) more time(s), ending with Row 5 of cable patt and substituting St st for the seed ridge patt in the final row to create a symmetrical patt arrangement with the start of the right sleeve—15 sts rem for all sizes; sleeve measures 8¼ (9, 9¾, 11¼, 12¼)" (21 [23, 25, 28.5, 31] cm) from marked row at end of left shoulder.

BO all sts with WS facing.

BACK

Left Sleeve, Left Underarm, Left Side, and Left Shoulder

Work as for front right sleeve, underarm, side, and shoulder to start of neck shaping, ending with RS Row 1 of patts—117 (123, 129, 135, 141) sts total; 12 cable sts at each side; 93 (99, 105, 111, 117) center sts in seed ridge patt; piece measures 4½ (5¼, 5¼, 6¼, 6¼)" (11.5 [13.5, 13.5, 16, 16] cm) from marked shoulder row and 6¼ (7, 7, 8, 8)" (16 [18, 18, 20.5, 20.5] cm) from sts CO at side.

Back Neck

Mark cable edge of last row completed to indicate start of back neck. Work 51 (51, 57, 57, 63) rows even, ending with WS Row 4 of patts.

Mark cable edge of last row completed for end of back neck—piece measures 6¾ (6¾, 7½, 7½, 8¼)" (17 [17, 19, 19, 21] cm) between neck markers.

Right Shoulder, Right Side, Right Underarm, and Right Sleeve

Work as for front left shoulder, side, underarm, and lower sleeve, ending with Row 5 of cable patt—15 sts rem for all sizes.

BO all sts with WS facing.

FINISHING

Weave in loose ends. Lightly steam-block pieces to measurements.

Sleeve Cuff (make 2)

CO 70 (74, 78, 82, 86) sts.

ROW 1: (RS) K2, *p2, k2; rep from *.

ROW 2: (WS) P2, *k2, p2; rep from *.

Rep the last 2 rows until piece measures 12 (12, 12, 13, 13)" (30.5 [30.5, 30.5, 33, 33] cm) from CO.

BO all sts.

Make a second cuff the same as the first.

Collar

CO 28 sts for all sizes.

SET-UP ROW: (WS) K4, p4, k4, pm, k16.

NEXT ROW: (RS) K16, sl m, work Row 1 of cable patt over last 12 sts.

Keeping sts outside cable in garter st (knit every row), cont in patt until piece measures about 19 (19, 21, 21, 22½)" (48.5 [48.5, 53.5, 53.5, 57] cm) from CO, ending with RS Row 1 of cable patt. BO all sts.

With yarn threaded on a tapestry needle, sew front to back at shoulders. Sew short underarm seams. Sew side and sleeve seams, starting at lower edge, working up the side of the body, and then down the sleeve to the marker indicating end of sleeve seams. Sew sleeve cuffs into tubes, then sew BO edge of each cuff to the sleeve opening, easing to fit. Sew CO to BO edges of collar to form a ring. Sew cable edge of collar to neck opening with collar seam centered at back neck.

As I walked along a busy New York street one crisp fall day, I noticed a short tailored jacket with an asymmetrical front. I was so enthralled that I stopped on the spot to sketch ideas for translating it into knitwear. This jacket is an ideal introduction to the main techniques I use for sideways knits—short-row shaping combined with increases and decreases on an effortless stockinette-stitch backdrop. The generous flared sleeves add a welcome bit of drama.

BECCA

FINISHED SIZE

About 30 (31, 32, 34, 35)" (76 [78.5, 81.5, 86.5, 89] cm) underbust circumference and 35 (39, 43, 47, 51)" (89 [99, 109, 119.5, 129.5] cm) full bust circumference, buttoned.

Sweater shown measures 30" (76 cm) at underbust and 35" (89 cm) at full bust.

YARN

Worsted Weight (#4 Medium).

Shown here: Brown Sheep Lamb's Pride Worsted (85% wool; 15% mohair; 190 yd [174 m]/4 oz [113.5 g]): #M26 medieval red, 7 (8, 9, 10, 11) skeins.

NEEDLES

Body and sleeves: size U.S. 9 (5.5 mm).

Edgings: size U.S. 7 (4.5 mm).

Adjust needle size if necessary to obtain the correct gauge.

NOTIONS

Tapestry needle; removable markers or waste yarn; five ¾" (2 cm) buttons.

GAUGE

16 sts and 24 rows = 4" (10 cm) in St st on larger needles.

BACK

With larger needles, CO 30 (32, 34, 36, 38) sts.

Shape Left Shoulder

Purl 1 WS row. Work short-rows (see Glossary) as foll:

ROWS 1, 3, 5, AND 7: (RS) Knit.

ROW 2: (WS) P6, wrap next st, turn work.

ROW 4: P12 while working wrap tog with previous wrapped st, wrap next st, turn.

ROW 6: P18 while working wrap tog with previous wrapped st, wrap next st, turn.

ROW 8: P24 while working wrap tog with previous wrapped st, wrap next st, turn.

ROW 9: Knit.

Cont according to your size as foll.

Sizes 35 (39, 43)" full bust only

ROW 10: (WS) Purl across all sts while working wrap tog with previous wrapped st—piece measures 1¾" (4.5 cm) from CO at shoulder edge (end of RS rows) and ½" (1.3 cm) at underarm edge (beg of RS rows).

Sizes (47, 51)" full bust only

ROW 10: (WS) P30 while working wrap tog with previous wrapped st, wrap next st, turn.

ROW 11: Knit to end.

ROW 12: Purl across all sts while working wrap tog with previous wrapped st—piece measures 2" (5 cm) from CO at shoulder edge (end of RS rows) and ½" (1.3 cm) at underarm edge (beg of RS rows).

Shape Left Underarm

With RS facing, mark the beg of last row completed to indicate start of underarm shaping at underarm edge.

ROW 1: (RS) K2, M1 (see Glossary), knit to end—1 st inc'd at underarm.

ROW 2: (WS) Purl.

ROW 3: K2, M1, knit to last 2 sts, M1, k2—2 sts inc'd: 1 st at underarm and 1 st at shoulder.

ROW 4: Purl.

Rep these 4 rows 1 (2, 3, 4, 5) more time(s)—36 (41, 46, 51, 56) sts; piece measures 3 (3¾, 4½, 5¼, 6)" (7.5 [9.5, 11.5, 13.5, 15] cm) from CO at shoulder and 1¼ (2, 2¾, 3¼, 4)" (3.2 [5, 7, 8.5, 10] cm) from marked row at underarm.

Body

NEXT ROW: (RS) Use the knitted method (see Glossary) to CO 30 (32, 34, 36, 38) sts at beg of row for left side, knit across new sts, then knit to end—66 (73, 80, 87, 94) sts total.

Purl 1 WS row.

ROW 1: (RS) Knit to last 2 sts, M1, k2—1 st inc'd at shoulder.

ROWS 2-4: Work 3 rows in St st, beg and ending with a WS row.

Rep the last 4 rows 5 (5, 6, 6, 7) more times, then work Row 1 once more—73 (80, 88, 95, 103) sts. Work even in St st for about ½ (½, 0, ½, 0)" (1.3 [1.3, 0, 1.3, 0] cm) after last inc row or until piece measures 5 (5, 5¼, 5¾, 5¾)" (12.5 [12.5, 13.5, 14.5, 14.5] cm) from sts CO at side.

Mark each end of last row completed to indicate end of left shoulder.

Work even in St st until back neck measures 5 (5½, 5½, 5½, 6)" (12.5 [14, 14, 14, 15] cm) from marked row at end of shoulder, ending with a WS row.

Mark each end of last row completed to indicate end of back neck.

Work even in St st until piece measures ½ (½, 0, ½, 0)" (1.3 [1.3, 0, 1.3, 0] cm) from marked row at end of back neck, ending with a WS row.

Cont as foll:

ROW 1: (RS) Knit to last 3 sts, k2tog, k1—1 st dec'd at shoulder.

ROWS 2-4: Work 3 rows even in St st, beg and ending with a WS row.

Rep these 4 rows 5 (5, 6, 6, 7) more times, then work Row 1 once more—66 (73, 80, 87, 94) sts rem.

Purl 1 WS row.

NEXT ROW: (RS) BO 30 (32, 34, 36, 38) sts, knit to end—36 (41, 46, 51, 56) sts rem; piece measures 15 (15½, 16, 17, 17½)" (38 [39.5, 40.5, 43, 44.5] cm) between sts CO and BO for sides.

Shape Right Underarm

ROW 1: (WS) Purl.

ROW 2: (RS) K1, ssk, knit to last 3 sts, k2tog, k1—2 sts dec'd: 1 st at underarm and 1 st at shoulder.

ROW 3: (WS) Purl.

ROW 4: K2, ssk, knit to end—1 st dec'd at underarm.

Rep these 4 rows 1 (2, 3, 4, 5) more time(s)—30 (32, 34, 36, 38) sts rem; piece measures 1¼ (2, 2¾, 3¼, 4)" (3.2 [5, 7, 8.5, 10] cm) from sts BO at right side and 17½ (19½, 21½, 23½, 25½)" (44.5 [49.5, 54.5, 59.5, 65] cm) from marked row at start of left underarm shaping.

NOTE: The distance between the beginning of the left underarm shaping and the end of the right underarm shaping is the width at the bustline when the garment is worn.

Shape Right Shoulder

Work according to your size as foll.

Sizes 35 (39, 43)" Full Bust Only

Purl 1 WS row. Skip to All Sizes.

Sizes (47, 51)" Full Bust Only

Purl 1 WS row, then knit 1 RS row.

NEXT ROW: (WS) P30, wrap next st, turn.

All Sizes

Work short-rows as foll:

ROWS 1, 3, 5, 7, AND 9: (RS) Knit.

ROW 2: (WS) P24, wrap next st, turn.

ROW 4: P18, wrap next st, turn.

ROW 6: P12, wrap next st, turn.

ROW 8: P6, wrap next st, turn.

ROW 10: Purl across all sts, working wraps tog with wrapped sts—piece measures 3 (3¾, 4½, 5¼, 6)" (7.5 [9.5, 11.5, 13.5, 15] cm) from sts BO for side at shoulder edge.

BO all sts.

RIGHT FRONT

With larger needles, CO 30 (32, 34, 36, 38) sts.

Shape Right Shoulder and Underarm

Work as for the back left shoulder and underarm, ending with a WS row—36 (41, 46, 51, 56) sts; piece measures 3 (3¾, 4½, 5¼, 6)" (7.5 [9.5, 11.5, 13.5, 15] cm) from CO at shoulder edge and 1¼ (2, 2¾, 3¼, 4)" (3.2 [5, 7, 8.5, 10] cm) from marked row at underarm.

Body

Work as for back body until piece measures 5 (5, 5¼, 5¾, 5¾)" (12.5 [12.5, 13.5, 14.5, 14.5] cm) from sts CO at side, ending with a RS row—73 (80, 88, 95, 103) sts.

Shape Neck

With WS facing, BO 9 (10, 11, 12, 13) sts, purl to end—64 (70, 77, 83, 90) sts rem.

DEC ROW: (RS) Knit to last 3 sts, k2tog, k1—1 st dec'd.

Cont in St st, rep the neck dec row on the next 2 (3, 4, 5, 6) RS rows, then work 1 WS row even—61 (66, 72, 77, 83) sts rem; neck measures about 1¼ (1½, 1¾, 2¼, 2½)" (3.2 [3.8, 4.5, 5.5, 6.5] cm) from BO row at start of neck shaping.

Shape Asymmetrical Front

Mark each end of last row completed to indicate beg of front shaping. Work short-rows as foll:

ROW 1: (RS) Knit.

ROW 2: (WS) P55 (60, 66, 71, 77) to last 6 sts, wrap next st, turn work.

ROW 3: Knit to end.

ROW 4: Purl to 5 sts before previous wrapped st, wrap next st, turn.

ROW 5: Knit to end.

Rep the last 2 rows 9 (10, 12, 13, 14) more times.

NEXT ROW: (WS) Purl across all sts, working the wraps tog with the wrapped sts—asymmetrical shaping measures 4 (4¼, 5, 5¼, 5¾)" (10 [11, 12.5, 13.5, 14.5] cm) from marked row at beg of front shaping along neck edge (end of RS rows) and ¼" (6 mm) from marked row at lower edge (beg of RS rows); piece measures 5¼ (5¾, 6¾, 7½, 8¼)" (13.5 [14.5, 17, 19, 21] cm) from first neck BO row at neck edge and 6½ (6¾, 7¼, 8¼, 8½)" (16.5 [17, 18.5, 21, 21.5] cm) from sts CO at side at lower edge.

Buttonhole Band

Change to smaller needles. Knit 4 rows even—2 garter ridges on RS.

BUTTONHOLE ROW: (RS) K11 (13, 16, 15, 18), [k2tog, yo, k13 (14, 15, 17, 18)] 3 times, k2tog, yo, k3—4 buttonholes.

NOTE: The 5th buttonhole will be worked in the lower edge ribbing.

Knit 4 rows, ending with a RS row—2 more garter ridges on RS; 4 garter ridges total; buttonhole band measures about 1¼" (3.2 cm) from last St st row of front.

With WS facing, loosely BO all sts knitwise.

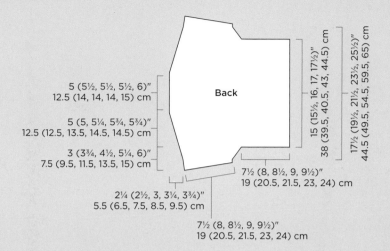

Back

5 (5½, 5½, 5½, 6)"
12.5 (14, 14, 14, 15) cm

5 (5, 5¼, 5¾, 5¾)"
12.5 (12.5, 13.5, 14.5, 14.5) cm

3 (3¾, 4½, 5¼, 6)"
7.5 (9.5, 11.5, 13.5, 15) cm

15 (15½, 16, 17, 17½)"
38 (39.5, 40.5, 43, 44.5) cm

17½ (19½, 21½, 23½, 25½)"
44.5 (49.5, 54.5, 59.5, 65) cm

7½ (8, 8½, 9, 9½)"
19 (20.5, 21.5, 23, 24) cm

2¼ (2½, 3, 3¼, 3¾)"
5.5 (6.5, 7.5, 8.5, 9.5) cm

7½ (8, 8½, 9, 9½)"
19 (20.5, 21.5, 23, 24) cm

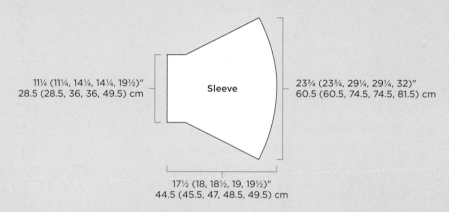

Sleeve

11¼ (11¼, 14¼, 14¼, 19½)"
28.5 (28.5, 36, 36, 49.5) cm

23¾ (23¾, 29¼, 29¼, 32)"
60.5 (60.5, 74.5, 74.5, 81.5) cm

17½ (18, 18½, 19, 19½)"
44.5 (45.5, 47, 48.5, 49.5) cm

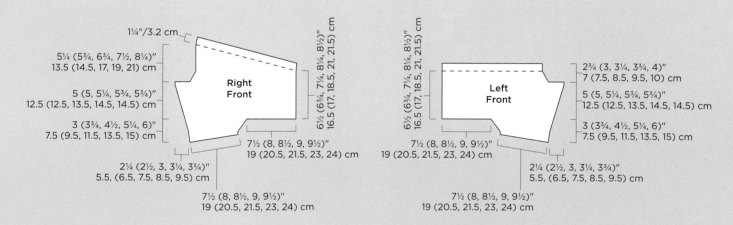

Right Front

1¼"/3.2 cm

5¼ (5¾, 6¾, 7½, 8¼)"
13.5 (14.5, 17, 19, 21) cm

5 (5, 5¼, 5¾, 5¾)"
12.5 (12.5, 13.5, 14.5, 14.5) cm

3 (3¾, 4½, 5¼, 6)"
7.5 (9.5, 11.5, 13.5, 15) cm

6½ (6¾, 7¼, 8¼, 8½)"
16.5 (17, 18.5, 21, 21.5) cm

7½ (8, 8½, 9, 9½)"
19 (20.5, 21.5, 23, 24) cm

2¼ (2½, 3, 3¼, 3¾)"
5.5, (6.5, 7.5, 8.5, 9.5) cm

7½ (8, 8½, 9, 9½)"
19 (20.5, 21.5, 23, 24) cm

Left Front

6½ (6¾, 7¼, 8¼, 8½)"
16.5 (17, 18.5, 21, 21.5) cm

2¾ (3, 3¼, 3¾, 4)"
7 (7.5, 8.5, 9.5, 10) cm

5 (5, 5¼, 5¾, 5¾)"
12.5 (12.5, 13.5, 14.5, 14.5) cm

3 (3¾, 4½, 5¼, 6)"
7.5 (9.5, 11.5, 13.5, 15) cm

7½ (8, 8½, 9, 9½)"
19 (20.5, 21.5, 23, 24) cm

2¼ (2½, 3, 3¼, 3¾)"
5.5, (6.5, 7.5, 8.5, 9.5) cm

7½ (8, 8½, 9, 9½)"
19 (20.5, 21.5, 23, 24) cm

LEFT FRONT

With larger needles, CO 30 (32, 34, 36, 38) sts.

Shape Left Shoulder

Purl 1 WS row. Work short-rows as foll:

ROW 1: (RS) K6, wrap next st, turn work.

ROWS 2, 4, AND 6: (WS) Purl.

ROW 3: K12 while working wrap tog with previous wrapped st, wrap next st, turn.

ROW 5: K18 while working wrap tog with previous wrapped st, wrap next st, turn.

ROW 7: K24 while working wrap tog with previous wrapped st, wrap next st, turn.

ROW 8: Purl.

Cont according to your size as foll.

Sizes 35 (39, 43)" Full Bust Only

ROW 9: (RS) Knit across all sts while working wrap tog with previous wrapped st.

Purl 1 WS row—piece measures 1¾" (4.5 cm) from CO at shoulder edge (beg of RS rows) and ½" (1.3 cm) at underarm edge (end of RS rows).

Sizes (47, 51)" Full Bust Only

ROW 9: (RS) K30 while working wrap tog with previous wrapped st, wrap next st, turn.

ROW 10: Purl.

ROW 11: Knit across all sts while working wrap tog with previous wrapped st.

Purl 1 WS row—piece measures 2" (5 cm) from CO at shoulder edge (beg of RS rows) and ½" (1.3 cm) at underarm edge (end of RS rows).

Shape Left Underarm

With RS facing, mark the end of last row completed to indicate start of underarm shaping at underarm edge.

ROW 1: (RS) Knit to last 2 sts, M1, k2—1 st inc'd at underarm.

ROW 2: (WS) Purl.

ROW 3: K2, M1, knit to last 2 sts, M1, k2—2 sts inc'd: 1 st at shoulder and 1 st at underarm.

ROW 4: Purl.

Rep these 4 rows 1 (2, 3, 4, 5) more time(s)—36 (41, 46, 51, 56) sts; piece measures 3 (3¾, 4½, 5¼, 6)" (7.5 [9.5, 11.5, 13.5, 15] cm) from CO at shoulder and 1¼ (2, 2¾, 3¼, 4)" (3.2 [5, 7, 8.5, 10] cm) from marked row at underarm.

Body

Knit 1 RS row.

NEXT ROW: (WS) Use the knitted method to CO 30 (32, 34, 36, 38) sts at beg of row for left side, purl across new sts, then purl to end—66 (73, 80, 87, 94) sts.

ROW 1: (RS) K2, M1, knit to end—1 st inc'd at shoulder.

ROWS 2-4: Work 3 rows in St st, beg and ending with a WS row.

Rep the last 4 rows 5 (5, 6, 6, 7) more times, then work Row 1 once more—73 (80, 88, 95, 103) sts.

Work even in St st until piece measures 5 (5, 5¼, 5¾, 5¾)" (12.5 [12.5, 13.5, 14.5, 14.5] cm) from sts CO at side along lower edge (end of RS rows), ending with a WS row.

Shape Neck

With RS facing, BO 9 (10, 11, 12, 13) sts, knit to end—64 (70, 77, 83, 90) sts rem.

Purl 1 WS row.

DEC ROW: (RS) K1, ssk, knit to end—1 st dec'd.

Cont in St st, rep the neck dec row on the next 2 (3, 4, 5, 6) RS rows, ending with the last RS dec row—61 (66, 72, 77, 83) sts rem; neck shaping measures about 1¼ (1½, 1¾, 2¼, 2½)" (3.2 [3.8, 4.5, 5.5, 6.5] cm) from neck BO row.

Work even in St st until piece measures 6½ (6¾, 7¼, 8¼, 8½)" (16.5 [17, 18.5, 21, 21.5] cm) from sts CO for side along lower edge, ending with a RS row.

Buttonband

Change to smaller needles. Knit 8 rows, ending with a RS row—4 garter ridges; band measures about 1¼" (3.2 cm) from last St st row of front.

With WS facing, loosely BO all sts kwise.

SLEEVES

With larger needles, CO 70 (72, 74, 76, 78) sts. Purl 1 WS row.

Shape Bell

Work 6 (6, 8, 8, 10) rows even in St st, ending with a WS row.

Work short-rows in Rev St st (knit RS rows; purl WS rows) as foll:

ROW 1: (RS) P14, wrap next st, turn work.

ROWS 2, 4, AND 6: (WS) Knit to end.

ROWS 3, 5, AND 7: Purl to wrapped st, work wrap tog with previously wrapped st as a purl st, p14, wrap next st, turn—with RS facing, wrapped st in Row 7 is the 60th st of the row for all sizes; 10 (12, 14, 16, 18) St sts rem unworked at end of row after last wrapped st.

ROW 8: Knit to end—14 (14, 16, 16, 18) rows of bell shaping measure about 2¼ (2¼, 2¾, 2¾, 3)" (5.5 [5.5, 7, 7, 7.5] cm) at belled lower edge (beg of RS rows) and 1 (1, 1¼, 1¼, 1¾)" (2.5 [2.5, 3.2, 3.2, 4.5] cm) at armhole edge (end of RS rows).

Rep the last 14 (14, 16, 16, 18) rows 9 more times, then work 7 (7, 9, 9, 11) rows even in St st, ending with a RS row—piece measures about 23¾ (23¾, 29¼, 29¼, 32)" (60.5 [60.5, 74.5, 74.5, 81.5] cm) from CO at lower edge and 11¼ (11¼, 14¼, 14¼, 19½)" (28.5 [28.5, 36, 36, 49.5] cm) at armhole edge.

Loosely BO all sts.

FINISHING

Weave in loose ends. With yarn threaded on a tapestry needle, sew fronts to back at shoulders.

Lower Edgings

Right Front

With smaller needles and RS facing, pick up and knit 36 (36, 40, 44, 44) sts evenly spaced along lower edge of right front.

NEXT ROW: (WS) *K2, p2; rep from * to end.

NEXT ROW: (RS) Work in established rib (knit the knits and purl the purls) to last 6 sts, p2tog, yo, k2, p2—5th buttonhole completed.

Work even in rib for 7 more rows, ending with a WS row.

Loosely BO all sts.

Left Front

With smaller needles and RS facing, pick up and knit 36 (36, 40, 44, 44) sts evenly spaced along lower edge of left front.

NEXT ROW: (WS) *P2, k2; rep from * to end.

Work even in established rib for 8 more rows, ending with a WS row.

Loosely BO all sts.

Back

With smaller needles and RS facing, pick up and knit 58 (62, 62, 66, 70) sts evenly spaced along lower edge of back.

NEXT ROW: (WS) P2, *k2, p2; rep from * to end.

Work even in rib for 8 more rows, ending with a WS row.

Loosely BO all sts.

Sew side and edging seams.

Cuffs

With smaller needles and RS facing, pick up and knit 118 (118, 145, 145, 159) sts evenly spaced along wide belled edge of sleeve. Knit 9 rows, beg and ending with a WS row—5 garter ridges on RS.

With RS facing, loosely BO all sts.

Sew sleeve and cuff seams. Sew sleeves into armholes, easing to fit.

Collar

With smaller needles, RS facing, and beg at BO edge of right front band, pick up and knit 17 (18, 19, 20, 21) sts along selvedge at top of band and assymmetrical shaping, 13 (15, 17, 19, 21) sts along right front neck shaping, 28 (30, 32, 34, 36) sts across back neck, 13 (15, 17, 19, 21) sts along left front neck shaping, and 11 (12, 13, 14, 15) sts along neck and band selvedge to BO edge of left front—82 (90, 98, 106, 114) sts total. Work in k2, p2 rib as for back lower edging until piece measures 8" (20.5 cm) from pick-up row, ending with a WS row.

With RS facing, BO all sts in rib patt.

Steam-block lightly, taking care to press seams nice and flat. Sew buttons to left front, opposite buttonholes.

As I began swatching for this piece, the idea for a tailored collar, flared sleeves, and short minimal body solidified into a design for a jacket that's perfect for layering. The sleek shaping is finessed with some subtle short-rows that produce pleasing drape in the collar and sleeves. The tailored sleeve caps are achieved with increases and decreases. Worn open, the jacket swings pleasantly with each step. Alternatively, it could be fastened with a brooch or zipper.

DEILLE

FINISHED SIZE

35 (38, 41, 44, 47)" (89 [96.5, 104, 112, 119.5] cm) bust circumference, with fronts meeting at center.

Sweater shown measures 35" (89 cm).

YARN

Worsted weight (#4 Medium).

Shown here: Noro Silk Garden (45% silk, 45% kid mohair, 10% wool; 108 yd [99 m]/50 g): #269, 10 (12, 13, 14, 16) balls.

NEEDLES

Size U.S. 7 (4.5 mm).

Adjust needle size if necessary to obtain the correct gauge.

NOTIONS

Cable needle (cn); markers (m); tapestry needle.

GAUGE

19 sts and 30 rows = 4" (10 cm) in both moss st and double garter st.

10 sts of cable patt measure 1¼" (3.2 cm) wide.

stitch guide

MOSS STITCH (EVEN NUMBER OF STS)

Row 1: (RS) *K1, p1; rep from *.

Rows 2 (WS) and 3 (RS): *P1, k1; rep from *.

Row 4: *K1, p1; rep from *.

Rep Rows 1–4 for pattern.

MOSS STITCH (ODD NUMBER OF STS)

Row 1: (RS) P1, *k1, p1; rep from *.

Rows 2 (WS) and 3 (RS): K1, *p1, k1; rep from *.

Row 4: P1, *k1, p1; rep from *.

Rep Rows 1–4 for pattern.

DOUBLE GARTER STITCH

Row 1: (RS) Purl.

Rows 2 (WS) and 3 (RS): Knit.

Row 4: Purl.

Rep Rows 1–4 for pattern.

CABLE PANEL (WORKED OVER 10 STS)

Set-up row: (WS) K2, p6, k2.

Row 1: (RS) P2, sl 3 sts onto cable needle (cn) and hold in back of work, k3, k3 from cn, p2.

Row 2: K2, p6, k2.

Row 3: P2, k6, p2.

Row 4: Rep Row 2.

Rep Rows 1–4 for pattern; do not rep Set-up row.

CUFF SHORT-ROWS

Row 1: (RS) Work 10 cable sts, sl m, p7 (8, 9, 10, 11), wrap next st, turn.

Rows 2 and 4: (WS) Knit to m, sl m, work 10 cable sts.

Rows 3 and 5: Work 10 cable sts, sl m, purl to previously wrapped st, work wrap tog with wrapped st, p7, wrap next st, turn—last wrapped st in Row 5 is the 34 (35, 36, 37, 38)th st from beg of row.

Row 6: Rep Row 2.

Row 7: (RS) Work 10 cable sts, work in established patt to last 10 sts, working rem wrap tog with wrapped st, work 10 cable sts.

Note: Every 7 cuff short-rows add about 1" (2.5 cm) to length of piece at cuff edge (beg of RS rows), and 1 row in height to rest of sleeve.

SINGLE INC ROW

On RS rows, work in patt to last 11 sts, k1f&b, sl m, work 10 cable sts—1 st inc'd for sleeve cap.

DOUBLE INC ROW

On RS rows, work in patt to last 11 sts, k1f&b, M1 (see Glossary) sl m, work 10 cable sts—2 sts inc'd for sleeve cap.

SINGLE DEC ROW

On RS rows, work in patt to last 12 sts, work next 2 sts tog as either k2tog or p2tog to maintain patt, sl m, work 10 cable sts—1 st dec'd for sleeve cap.

DOUBLE DEC ROW

On RS rows, work in patt to last 13 sts, work next 3 sts tog as either k3tog or p3tog to maintain patt, sl m, work 10 cable sts—2 sts dec'd for sleeve cap.

notes

+ The back is worked sideways in two halves that are seamed together, each half beginning at center back and worked outwards to the side seam. Each front is worked from the center of the body to the side seam with short-rows to shape the lapel.

+ The right side of the collar cables corresponds to the wrong side of the body so that the right side of these cables will show when the collar and lapels are folded back. Because of this, the collar cables will not be on the same pattern row as the lower edge cables; keep track of the cable patterns individually.

+ The sleeves are worked sideways by casting on for the length of the sleeve seam, then working around the arm with stitches added and removed to shape the sleeve cap and with short-rows to shape the belled cuffs. The sleeves are sewn into the armholes during finishing.

RIGHT BACK

Center Back and Collar

CO 120 (128, 134, 140, 146) sts.

SET-UP ROW: (WS of body, RS of collar cable; see Notes) Work RS Row 1 of cable panel (see Stitch Guide) over first 10 sts at collar edge, place marker (pm), *k1, p1; rep from * to last 10 sts, pm, work WS set-up row of cable panel over last 10 sts at lower edge.

NEXT ROW: (RS of body, WS of collar cable) Work RS Row 1 of cable panel over first 10 sts, work Row 1 of moss st (see Stitch Guide) over center 100 (108, 114, 120, 126) sts, work WS Row 2 of cable panel over last 10 sts.

Cont in established patts until piece measures 3½ (3½, 3½, 4, 4)" (9 [9, 9, 10, 10] cm) from CO, ending with a RS body row.

Work short-rows (see Glossary) to shape collar as foll:

ROW 1: (WS of body, RS of collar cable) Work 10 cable sts, slip marker (sl m), p10 (14, 18, 22, 26) wrap next st, turn work.

ROWS 2 AND 4: (RS of body, WS of collar cable) Knit to last 10 sts, sl m, work 10 cable sts.

ROWS 3 AND 5: Work 10 cable sts, sl m, purl to 1 st before previously wrapped st, wrap next st, turn.

ROW 6: Rep Row 2—piece measures 4¼ (4¼, 4¼, 4¾, 4¾)" (11 [11, 11, 12, 12] cm) from CO at collar edge (end of RS body rows); no change to length at lower edge (beg of RS rows).

NEXT ROW: (WS of body) Working wraps tog with wrapped sts as you come to them, BO 20 (22, 22, 24, 26) sts, work in patt to last 10 sts, sl m, work 10 cable sts—100 (106, 112, 116, 120) sts rem.

Shape Shoulder

Work 2 rows even in patt, ending with a WS row.

DEC ROW: (RS) Work in patt to last 3 sts, work k2tog or p2tog as necessary to maintain patt, work last st in patt—1 st dec'd.

Work 3 rows even in patt, beg and ending with a WS row.

Rep the last 4 rows 4 (4, 5, 5, 5) more times, ending with a WS row—95 (101, 106, 110, 114) sts; piece measures 6½ (6½, 7, 7½, 7½)" (16.5 [16.5, 18, 19, 19] cm) from CO at lower edge; shoulder measures 3 (3, 3½, 3½, 3½)" (7.5 [7.5, 9, 9, 9] cm) from collar BO measured straight up along a single column of sts; do not measure along sloped shoulder selvedge.

Work short-rows as foll:

ROW 1: (RS) Work even in patt.

ROW 2: (WS) K5, wrap next st, turn.

ROW 3: (RS) Purl to end.

ROW 4: Knit to previously wrapped st, work wrap tog with wrapped st, k5, wrap next st, turn.

ROW 5: Purl to end.

Rep the last 2 rows 1 (2, 2, 3, 3) more time(s)—wrapped st in last WS short-row is the 18 (24, 24, 30, 30)th st of the row; shoulder measures 4 (4¼, 4¾, 5, 5)" (10 [11, 12, 12.5, 12.5] cm) from collar BO at shoulder edge; no change to length measurement at lower edge.

Shape Armhole

With WS facing, BO 30 (31, 33, 35, 37) sts, work in patt to end—65 (70, 73, 75, 77) sts rem.

DEC ROW: (RS) Work 10 cable sts, sl m, work Row 1 of double garter st (see Stitch Guide) to last 3 sts, work p2tog or k2tog as needed to maintain patt, work last st in patt—1 st dec'd.

Work 1 WS row even in patt.

Cont in patt, rep the last 2 rows 2 (4, 4, 4, 5) more times, ending with a WS row—62 (65, 68, 70, 71) sts rem.

Cont in established patts until piece measures 8½ (9, 9½, 10, 10½)" (21.5 [23, 24, 25.5, 26.5] cm) from CO at lower edge, ending with a WS row.

BO all sts.

LEFT BACK
Center Back and Collar

CO 120 (128, 134, 140, 146) sts.

SET-UP ROW: (WS of body, RS of collar cable) Work WS Set-up row of cable panel over first 10 sts at lower edge, pm, *k1, p1; rep from * to last 10 sts, pm, work RS Row 1 of cable panel over last 10 sts at collar edge.

NEXT ROW: (RS of body, WS of collar cable) Work WS Row 2 of cable panel over first 10 sts, work Row 1 of moss st over center 100 (108, 114, 120, 126) sts, work RS Row 1 of cable panel over last 10 sts.

Cont in established patts until piece measures 3½ (3½, 3½, 4, 4)" (9 [9, 9, 10, 10] cm) from CO, ending with a WS body row.

Work short-rows to shape collar as foll:

ROW 1: (RS of body, WS of collar cable) Work 10 cable sts, sl m, k10 (14, 18, 22, 26), wrap next st, turn.

ROWS 2 AND 4: (WS of body, RS of collar cable) Purl to last 10 sts, sl m, work 10 cable sts.

ROWS 3 AND 5: Work 10 cable sts, sl m, knit to 1 st before previously wrapped st, wrap next st, turn.

ROW 6: Rep Row 2—piece measures 4¼ (4¼, 4¼, 4¾, 4¾)" (11 [11, 11, 12, 12] cm) from CO at collar edge (beg of RS body rows); no change to length at lower edge (end of RS rows).

NEXT ROW: (RS of body) Working wraps tog with wrapped sts as you come to them, BO 20 (22, 22, 24, 26) sts, work in patt to last 10 sts, sl m, work 10 cable sts—100 (106, 112, 116, 120) sts rem.

Shape Shoulder

Work 3 rows even in patt, beg and ending with a WS row.

DEC ROW: (RS) Work 1 st in patt, work next 2 sts as ssk or ssp (see Glossary) as necessary to maintain patt, work in patt to end—1 st dec'd.

Work 3 rows even in patt, beg and ending with a WS row.

Rep the last 4 rows 4 (4, 5, 5, 5) more times, ending with a WS row—95 (101, 106, 110, 114) sts; piece measures 6½ (6½, 7, 7½, 7½)" (16.5 [16.5, 18, 19, 19] cm) from CO at lower edge; shoulder measures about 3 (3, 3½, 3½, 3½)" (7.5 [7.5, 9, 9, 9] cm) from collar BO, measured straight up along a single column of sts; do not measure along sloped shoulder selvedge.

Work short-rows as foll:

ROW 1: (RS) P5, wrap next st, turn.

ROW 2: (WS) Knit to end.

ROW 3: Purl to previously wrapped st, work wrap tog with wrapped st, p5, wrap next st, turn.

ROW 4: Knit to end.

Rep the last 2 rows 1 (2, 2, 3, 3) more time(s)—wrapped st in last RS short-row is the 18 (24, 24, 30, 30)th st of the row; shoulder measures about 4 (4¼, 4¾, 5, 5)" (10 [11, 12, 12.5, 12.5] cm) from collar BO at shoulder edge; no change to length measurement at lower edge.

Shape Armhole

With RS facing, BO 30 (31, 33, 35, 37) sts, work Row 1 of double garter st to last 10 sts, sl m, work 10 cable sts—65 (70, 73, 75, 77) sts.

Work 1 WS row even in patt.

DEC ROW: (RS) Work 1 st in patt, work p2tog or k2tog as needed to maintain patt, work in patt to last 10 sts, work 10 cable sts—1 st dec'd.

NEXT ROW: (WS) Work even in patt.

NEXT ROW: (WS) BO 10 cable sts, remove m, work in patt to end—107 (114, 121, 128, 133) sts rem.

DEC ROW: (RS) Work in patt to last 3 sts, ssk, k1—1 st dec'd.

Work 1 WS row even in patt.

Rep the last 2 rows 6 (7, 8, 11, 12) more times, ending with a WS row—100 (106, 112, 116, 120) sts; piece measures 4 (4½, 5, 6, 6½)" (10 [11.5, 12.5, 15, 16.5] cm) from sts CO at center front.

Shape Shoulder

With RS facing, mark each end of last row completed to indicate start of shoulder section.

Work 2 rows even in patt, ending with a WS row.

DEC ROW: (RS) Work in patt to last 3 sts, work next 2 sts as k2tog or p2tog as necessary to maintain patt, work last st in patt—1 st dec'd.

Work 3 rows even in patt, beg and ending with a WS row.

Rep the last 4 rows 4 (4, 5, 5, 5) more times, ending with a WS row—95 (101, 106, 110, 114) sts rem; piece measures 3 (3, 3½, 3½, 3½)" (7.5 [7.5, 9, 9, 9] cm) from marked row and 7 (7½, 8½, 9½, 10)" (18 [19, 21.5, 24, 25.5] cm) from sts CO at center front.

Work short-rows as foll:

ROW 1: (RS) Work in patt to end.

ROW 2: (WS) K5, wrap next st, turn.

ROW 3: Purl to end.

ROW 4: Knit to previously wrapped st, work wrap tog with wrapped st, k5, wrap next st, turn.

ROW 5: Purl to end.

Rep the last 2 rows 1 (2, 2, 3, 3) more time(s)—wrapped st in last WS short-row is the 18 (24, 24, 30, 30)th st of the row; shoulder measures 4 (4¼, 4¾, 5, 5)" (10 [11, 12, 12.5, 12.5] cm) from marked row at shoulder edge (end of RS rows); no change to length measurement from sts CO at center front.

Shape Armhole

With WS facing, BO 30 (31, 33, 35, 37) sts, work in patt to end—65 (70, 73, 75, 77) sts rem.

DEC ROW: (RS) Work 10 cable sts, sl m, work Row 1 of double garter st to last 3 sts, work p2tog or k2tog as needed to maintain patt, work last st in patt—1 st dec'd.

NEXT ROW: (WS) Work even in patt.

Cont in patt, rep the last 2 rows 2 (4, 4, 4, 5) more times, ending with a WS row—62 (65, 68, 70, 71) sts rem.

Cont in established patts until piece measures 9 (10, 11, 12, 13)" (23 [25.5, 28, 30.5, 33] cm) from sts CO at center front, ending with a WS row.

BO all sts.

RIGHT FRONT
Lapel

CO 13 sts for all sizes.

SET-UP ROW: (WS of body, RS of collar cable) P3, pm, work RS Row 1 of cable panel over last 10 sts at collar edge.

ROW 1: (RS of body, WS of collar cable) Work WS Row 2 of cable over first 10 sts, [k1f&b] 2 times, k1—15 sts.

ROW 2: K1, [p1, k1] 2 times, work 10 cable sts.

ROW 3: Work 10 cable sts, k1f&b, work Row 1 of moss st to last 2 sts, k1f&b, k1—2 sts inc'd.

ROW 4: K1, work in moss st to last st, working new sts into moss st, work 10 cable sts.

Rep Rows 3 and 4 only 8 (9, 9, 10, 10) more times, ending with a WS row—33 (35, 35, 37, 37) sts; piece measures 2¾ (3, 3, 3¼, 3¼)" (7 [7.5, 7.5, 8.5, 8.5] cm) from CO, measured straight up along a single column of sts; do not measure along shaped selvedges.

Change the angle of the incs by working double incs at end of RS rows as foll:

INC ROW: (RS) Work 10 cable sts, k1f&b, work in moss st to last 2 sts, knit into the front, back, and front of next st (3 sts made from 1 st), k1—3 sts inc'd.

NEXT ROW: (WS) K1, work in moss st to last 10 sts, working new sts into moss st, work 10 cable sts.

Rep the last 2 rows 5 (6, 7, 8, 9) more times, ending with a WS row—51 (56, 59, 64, 67) sts; piece measures 4¼ (4¾, 5¼, 5¾, 6)" (11 [12, 13.5, 14.5, 15] cm) from CO.

Center Front and Collar

(RS) Work 10 cable sts, k1f&b, work in moss st to end, use the cable method to CO 58 (59, 62, 63, 64) sts at end of row—110 (116, 122, 128, 132) sts.

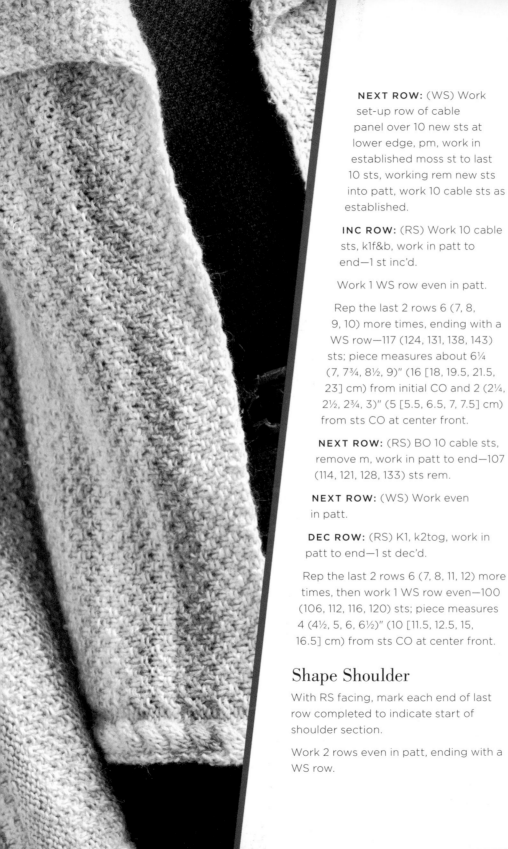

NEXT ROW: (WS) Work set-up row of cable panel over 10 new sts at lower edge, pm, work in established moss st to last 10 sts, working rem new sts into patt, work 10 cable sts as established.

INC ROW: (RS) Work 10 cable sts, k1f&b, work in patt to end—1 st inc'd.

Work 1 WS row even in patt.

Rep the last 2 rows 6 (7, 8, 9, 10) more times, ending with a WS row—117 (124, 131, 138, 143) sts; piece measures about 6¼ (7, 7¾, 8½, 9)" (16 [18, 19.5, 21.5, 23] cm) from initial CO and 2 (2¼, 2½, 2¾, 3)" (5 [5.5, 6.5, 7, 7.5] cm) from sts CO at center front.

NEXT ROW: (RS) BO 10 cable sts, remove m, work in patt to end—107 (114, 121, 128, 133) sts rem.

NEXT ROW: (WS) Work even in patt.

DEC ROW: (RS) K1, k2tog, work in patt to end—1 st dec'd.

Rep the last 2 rows 6 (7, 8, 11, 12) more times, then work 1 WS row even—100 (106, 112, 116, 120) sts; piece measures 4 (4½, 5, 6, 6½)" (10 [11.5, 12.5, 15, 16.5] cm) from sts CO at center front.

Shape Shoulder

With RS facing, mark each end of last row completed to indicate start of shoulder section.

Work 2 rows even in patt, ending with a WS row.

DEC ROW: (RS) Work 1 st in patt, work next 2 sts as ssk or ssp (see Glossary) as necessary to maintain patt, work in patt to end—1 st dec'd.

Work 3 rows even in patt, beg and ending with a WS row.

Rep the last 4 rows 4 (4, 5, 5, 5) more times, ending with a WS row—95 (101, 106, 110, 114) sts rem; piece measures 3 (3, 3½, 3½, 3½)" (7.5 [7.5, 9, 9, 9] cm) from marked row and 7 (7½, 8½, 9½, 10)" (18 [19, 21.5, 24, 25.5] cm) from sts CO at center front.

Work short-rows as foll:

ROW 1: (RS) P5, wrap next st, turn.

ROW 2: (WS) Knit to end.

ROW 3: Purl to previously wrapped st, work wrap tog with wrapped st, p5, wrap next st, turn.

ROW 4: Knit to end.

Rep the last 2 rows 1 (2, 2, 3, 3) more time(s)—wrapped st in last RS short-row is the 18 (24, 24, 30, 30)th st of the row; shoulder measures 4 (4¼, 4¾, 5, 5)" (10 [11, 12, 12.5, 12.5] cm) from marked row at shoulder edge (beg of RS rows); no change to length measurement from sts CO at center front.

Shape Armhole

With RS facing, BO 30 (31, 33, 35, 37) sts, work Row 1 of double garter st to last 10 sts, sl m, work 10 cable sts—65 (70, 73, 75, 77) sts rem.

Work 1 WS row even in patt.

DEC ROW: (RS) Work 1 st in patt, work p2tog or k2tog as needed to maintain patt, work in patt to last 10 sts, work 10 cable sts—1 st dec'd.

Work 1 WS row even in patt.

Cont in patt, rep the last 2 rows 2 (4, 4, 4, 5) more times, ending with a WS row—62 (65, 68, 70, 71) sts rem.

Cont in established patts until piece measures 9 (10, 11, 12, 13)" (23 [25.5, 28, 30.5, 33] cm) from CO at lower edge, ending with a WS row.

BO all sts.

SLEEVES

CO 85 (89, 93, 97, 101) sts.

SET-UP ROW: (WS) Work set-up row of cable panel over first 10 sts, pm, work moss st over center 65 (69, 73, 77, 81) sts beg with WS Row 4 of patt, pm, work set-up row of cable panel over last 10 sts.

Work cuff short-row sequence (see Stitch Guide), ending with a RS row— piece measures about 1" (2.5 cm) from CO at cuff edge (beg of RS rows) and ¼" (6 mm) in non-short-row section of sleeve.

Work a separate set of short-rows at sleeve cap edge (beg of WS rows) as foll:

ROW 1: (WS) Work 10 cable sts, sl m, k8 (9, 10, 11, 12), wrap next st, turn.

ROWS 2 AND 4: (RS) Purl to m, sl m, work 10 cable sts.

ROWS 3 AND 5: Work 10 cable sts, sl m, purl to previously wrapped st, work wrap tog with wrapped st, p7, wrap next st, turn.

ROW 6: Rep Row 2, ending with a RS row—piece measures about 1" (2.5 cm) from CO at both selvedges; no change to center section without short-rows.

NOTE: For the rest of the sleeve, work 9 rows across all sts (beginning and ending with a WS row) followed by 7 cuff short-rows (beginning and ending with a RS row). In each 16-row sequence, 10 rows will be worked across all sts: the first 9 rows, plus Row 7 of the cuff short-rows. The sleeve cap is shaped by increasing or decreasing inside the sleeve cap cable in the 10 rows of each 16-row sequence that extend all the way to the cap edge. Read the next sections all the way through before proceeding.

With RS facing, mark each end of last row completed. [Work 9 rows in patt across all sts, then work 7 cuff short-rows] 8 (9, 10, 10, 11) times, then work 9 rows in patt across all sts, ending with a WS row—137 (153, 169, 169, 185) rows at cuff edge in sleeve cap section; 89 (99, 109, 109, 119) rows at sleeve cap edge; 44 (49, 54, 54, 59) RS rows extending to sleeve cap edge available for shaping. *At the same time* work the first 4 (4, 4, 3, 3) RS rows even without shaping.

Work the next 4 (5, 5, 6, 6) RS rows as a single inc row (see Stitch Guide), then the foll 5 (6, 7, 7, 8) RS rows as a double inc row (see Stitch Guide), then the next 6 (6, 7, 7, 8) RS rows as a single inc row—105 (112, 119, 124, 131) sts.

Work the next 6 (7, 8, 8, 9) RS rows even, without shaping. Work the next 6 (6, 7, 7, 8) RS rows as a single dec row (see Stitch Guide), then the foll 5 (6, 7, 7, 8) RS rows as a double dec row (see Stitch Guide), then the next 4 (5, 5, 6, 6) RS rows as a single dec row—85 (89, 93, 97, 101) sts rem.

Work the last 4 (4, 4, 3, 3) RS rows even without shaping—44 (49, 54, 54, 59) RS rows.

With RS facing, mark each end of last row completed—piece measures 11¾ (13¼, 14½, 14½, 15¾)" (30 [33.5, 37, 37, 40] cm) between marked rows of sleeve cap.

Work a separate set of short-rows at sleeve cap edge as foll:

ROW 1: (RS) Work in patt to end.

ROW 2: (WS) Work 10 cable sts, sl m, k8 (9, 10, 11, 12), wrap next st, turn.

ROWS 3 AND 5: Purl to m, sl m, work 10 cable sts.

ROWS 4 AND 6: Work 10 cable sts, sl m, purl to previously wrapped st, work wrap tog with wrapped st, p7, wrap next st, turn.

ROW 7: Rep Row 3, ending with a RS row—piece measures about 1" (2.5 cm) from marked row at end of cap shaping at cap edge.

NEXT ROW: (WS) Work 1 row in patt across all sts, working wrap tog with wrapped st.

Work cuff short-row sequence, beg and ending with a RS row—piece measures about 20¾ (23¼, 25½, 25½, 27½)" (52.5 [59, 65, 65, 70] cm) from CO along cuff selvedge and 13¾ (15¼, 16½, 16½, 17¾)" (35 [38.5, 42, 42, 45] cm) from CO measured along a single column of sts at the upper arm, just below the cap shaping when the garment is worn.

Loosely BO all sts.

FINISHING

Weave in loose ends. Gently steam-block all pieces, taking care not to flatten cables or stretch the cable at the sleeve cap edge.

With yarn threaded on a tapestry needle, sew center back seam, reversing the top 3¼ (3¾, 3¾, 4¼, 4½)" (8.5 [9.5, 9.5, 11, 11.5] cm) of the seam in the collar section so that the RS of the collar seam allowance will show on the outside when the collar is folded back.

Sew fronts to back at shoulders, working from each armhole edge in toward the back collar BO corner. Sew the BO edge of each back collar to the shaped collar edge of front, reversing the seam allowances so the RS of these seams will show on the outside when the collar is folded back. Sew sleeve caps into armholes. Sew sleeve and side seams.

For this wearable top, I took inspiration from an Asian-inspired silk bolero that had flawless drape and a look of softness that belied the rather stiff fabric from which it was made. Worked in worsted-weight yarn, the simple embossed diamond stitch pattern is a nod to Asian tradition, but the stand-up collar, single button closure, and slightly flared hem update the overall look. Unlike most of the other sweaters in this book, Francesca has no cables.

FRANCESCA

FINISHED SIZE
About 36½ (39, 42, 46½, 50)" (92.5 [99, 106.5, 118, 127] cm) bust circumference, with 1" (2.5 cm) front edges overlapped. Sweater shown measures 39" (99 cm).

YARN
Worsted weight (#4 Medium).

Shown here: Mission Falls 1824 Wool (100% wool; 85 yd [78 m]/50 g): #013 curry, 10 (11, 13, 14, 17) balls.

NEEDLES
Edging: size U.S. 7 (4.5 mm).
Body and sleeves: size U.S. 9 (5.5 mm).
Adjust needle size if necessary to obtain the correct gauge.

NOTIONS
Markers (m); tapestry needle, one 1¼" (3.2 cm) button.

GAUGE
16½ sts and 27½ rows = 4" (10 cm) in diamond pattern (see Stitch Guide) on larger needles.

stitch guide

K2, P2 RIB (MULTIPLE OF 4 STS + 2)

Row 1: (RS) P2, *k2, p2; rep from *.

Row 2: (WS) K2, *p2, k2; rep from *.

Rep Rows 1 and 2 for pattern.

DIAMOND PATTERN FOR SWATCHING (MULTIPLE OF 6 STS + 1)

Row 1: (RS) P1, *k5, p1; rep from *.

Row 2: (WS) K1, *p5, k1; rep from *.

Row 3: K1, *p1, k3, p1, k1; rep from *.

Row 4: P1, *k1, p3, k1, p1; rep from *.

Row 5: K2, *p1, k1, p1, k3; rep from * to last 5 sts, p1, k1, p1, k2.

Row 6: P2, *k1, p1, k1, p3; rep from * to last 5 sts, k1, p1, k1, p2.

Row 7: K3, *p1, k5; rep from * to last 4 sts, p1, k3.

Row 8: P3, *k1, p5; rep from * to last 4 sts, k1, p3.

Rows 9 and 10: Rep Rows 5 and 6.

Rows 11 and 12: Rep Rows 3 and 4.

Rep Rows 1–12 for pattern.

notes

+ Each front is worked sideways from sleeve cuff to center front.

+ The back is worked in one piece from side to side, beginning at one sleeve cuff and ending at the other.

LEFT FRONT

Sleeve

With smaller needles, CO 30 (30, 34, 34, 38) sts. Work in k2, p2 rib (see Stitch Guide) for 8 rows—piece measures 1″ (2.5 cm) from CO.

Change to larger needles.

ROW 1: (RS) Work Row 1 of Left Front Sleeve chart (see page 46) over 28 (28, 32, 32, 36) sts, inc 1 st in chart as shown and ending where indicated for your size, k1f&b (see Glossary) in next st, k1—2 sts inc'd.

ROW 2: (WS) P2, then beg where indicated for your size, work Row 2 of chart to end.

ROWS 3, 5, 7, 9, AND 11: Work established chart patt to last 2 sts, inc 1 st in chart as shown and ending where indicated for your size, k1f&b, k1—2 sts inc'd each row.

ROWS 4, 6, 8, 10, AND 12: P2, beg where indicated for your size, work in chart patt to end—42 (42, 46, 46, 50) sts after completing Row 12.

ROW 13: Work Row 1 of chart over 40 (40, 44, 44, 48) sts, inc 1 st in chart as shown and ending where indicated for your size, k1f&b, k1—2 sts inc'd.

ROW 14: P2, beg where indicated for your size, work Row 2 of chart to end.

ROWS 15, 17, 19, 21, AND 23: Work established chart patt to last 2 sts, inc 1 st in chart as shown and ending where indicated for your size, k1f&b, k1—2 sts inc'd each row.

ROWS 16, 18, 20, 22, AND 24: P2, work in chart patt to end, beg where indicated for your size—54 (54, 58, 58, 62) sts after completing Row 24; last chart row completed is Row 12.

For the 3 largest sizes only, work additional rows as foll.

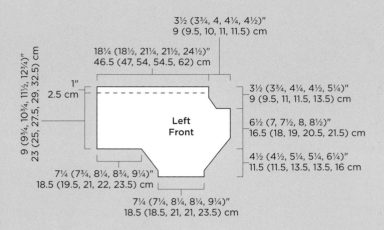

3½ (3¾, 4, 4¼, 4½)"
9 (9.5, 10, 11, 11.5) cm

18¼ (18½, 21¼, 21½, 24½)"
46.5 (47, 54, 54.5, 62) cm

9 (9¾, 10¾, 11½, 12¾)"
23 (25, 27.5, 29, 32.5) cm

1"
2.5 cm

Left
Front

3½ (3¾, 4¼, 4½, 5¼)"
9 (9.5, 11, 11.5, 13.5) cm

6½ (7, 7½, 8, 8½)"
16.5 (18, 19, 20.5, 21.5) cm

4½ (4½, 5¼, 5¼, 6¼)"
11.5 (11.5, 13.5, 13.5, 16) cm

7¼ (7¾, 8¼, 8¾, 9¼)"
18.5 (19.5, 21, 22, 23.5) cm

7¼ (7¼, 8¼, 8¼, 9¼)"
18.5 (18.5, 21, 21, 23.5) cm

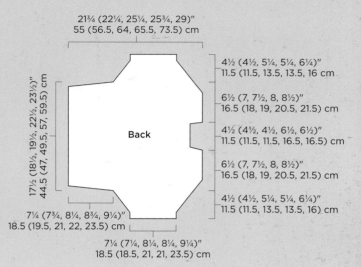

21¾ (22¼, 25¼, 25¾, 29)"
55 (56.5, 64, 65.5, 73.5) cm

17½ (18½, 19½, 22½, 23½)"
44.5 (47, 49.5, 57, 59.5) cm

Back

4½ (4½, 5¼, 5¼, 6¼)"
11.5 (11.5, 13.5, 13.5, 16) cm

6½ (7, 7½, 8, 8½)"
16.5 (18, 19, 20.5, 21.5) cm

4½ (4½, 4½, 6½, 6½)"
11.5 (11.5, 11.5, 16.5, 16.5) cm

6½ (7, 7½, 8, 8½)"
16.5 (18, 19, 20.5, 21.5) cm

4½ (4½, 5¼, 5¼, 6¼)"
11.5 (11.5, 13.5, 13.5, 16) cm

7¼ (7¾, 8¼, 8¾, 9¼)"
18.5 (19.5, 21, 22, 23.5) cm

7¼ (7¼, 8¼, 8¼, 9¼)"
18.5 (18.5, 21, 21, 23.5) cm

Sizes (42, 46½)" Only

ROW 25: Work Row 1 of chart over (56, 56) sts, inc 1 st in chart as shown and ending where indicated for your size, k1f&b, k1—2 sts inc'd.

ROW 26: P2, beg where indicated for your size, work Row 2 of chart to end.

ROWS 27 AND 29: Work established chart patt to last 2 sts, inc 1 st in chart as shown and ending where indicated for your size, k1f&b, k1—2 sts inc'd each row.

ROWS 28 AND 30: P2, beg where indicated for your size, work in chart patt to end—(64, 64) sts after completing Row 30; last chart row completed is Row 6.

Size 50" Only

ROW 25: Work Row 1 of chart over 60 sts, inc 1 st in chart as shown and ending where indicated for your size, k1f&b, k1—2 sts inc'd.

ROW 26: P2, beg where indicated for your size, work Row 2 of chart to end.

ROWS 27, 29, 31, 33, AND 35: Work established chart patt to last 2 sts, inc 1 st in chart as shown and ending where indicated for your size, k1f&b, k1— 2 sts inc'd each row.

ROWS 28, 30, 32, 34, AND 36: P2, beg where indicated for your size, work in chart patt to end—74 sts after completing Row 36; last chart row completed is Row 12.

All Sizes

Sleeve measures 4½ (4½, 5¼, 5¼, 6¼)" (11.5 [11.5, 13.5, 13.5, 16] cm) from CO—54 (54, 64, 64, 74) sts total.

Body

NOTE: Maintain 9 sts in established welt patt at shoulder (beg of RS rows, end of WS rows) until these sts are bound off for the neck shaping.

ROW 1: (RS) Cont in established patt, work 9 sts, M1P, work in patt to end, use the backward-loop method (see Glossary) to CO 30 (32, 34, 36, 38) sts for side—85 (87, 99, 101, 113) sts.

ROW 2: (WS) Work first 8 new sts as [p2, k2] 2 times for lower edge, place marker (pm), work in patt to end, working rem new CO sts into established diamond patt.

ROW 3: Work 9 sts in patt, M1P, work in patt to m, slip marker (sl m), [p2, k2] 2 times—1 st inc'd at shoulder only.

ROW 4: [P2, k2] 2 times, sl m, work in patt to end.

Rep the last 2 rows 4 (4, 5, 5, 6) more times—90 (92, 105, 107, 120) sts.

Discontinue incs at shoulder (beg of RS rows) and work even in established patt until body measures 6½ (7, 7½, 8, 8½)" (16.5 [18, 19, 20.5, 21.5] cm) from sts CO at side, ending with a WS row.

Key

□ knit on RS; purl on WS

▪ purl on RS; knit on WS

MP M1P (see Glossary)

□ pattern repeat

Left Front Sleeve

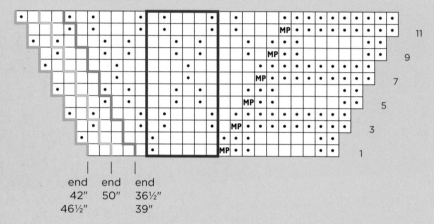

11
9
7
5
3
1

end 42"
46½"

end 50"

end 36½"
39"

Right Front Sleeve

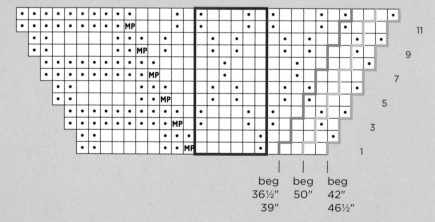

11
9
7
5
3
1

beg 36½"
39"

beg 50"

beg 42"
46½"

Shape Neck

BO 9 sts at beg of next RS row, work in patt to end—81 (83, 96, 98, 111) sts rem. Work 1 WS row even.

DEC ROW: (RS) K1, ssk, work in patt to end—1 st dec'd.

Work 1 WS row even.

Dec 1 st at neck edge in this manner on the next 5 (6, 7, 8, 9) RS rows, ending with the final RS dec row—75 (76, 88, 89, 101) sts.

Work 4 (4, 6, 6, 8) rows even in patt, ending with a RS row—body measures 2½ (2¾, 3¼, 3½, 4¼)" (6.5 [7, 8.5, 9, 11] cm) from start of neck shaping.

Front Edging

Change to smaller needles. *Purl 1 WS row, knit 2 rows, purl 1 RS row; rep from * once more—body measures 10 (10¾, 11¼, 12½, 13¾)" (25.5 [27.5, 30, 31.5, 35] cm) from sts CO at side; piece measures 14½ (15¼, 17, 17¾, 20)" (37 [38.5, 43, 45, 51] cm) from beg CO.

With WS facing, loosely BO all sts.

RIGHT FRONT
Sleeve

With smaller needles, CO 30 (30, 34, 34, 38) sts. Work in k2, p2 rib (see Stitch Guide) for 8 rows—piece measures 1" (2.5 cm) from CO.

Change to larger needles.

ROW 1: (RS) K1, k1f&b, then beg where indicated for your size work Row 1 of Right Front Sleeve chart over 28 (28, 32, 32, 36) sts, inc 1 st in chart as shown—2 sts inc'd.

ROW 2: (WS) Work Row 2 of chart to last 2 sts, ending where indicated for your size, p2.

ROWS 3, 5, 7, 9, AND 11: K1, k1f&b, beg where indicated for your size, work established chart patt to end, inc 1 st in chart as shown—2 sts inc'd each row.

ROWS 4, 6, 8, 10, AND 12: Work in chart patt to last 2 sts, ending where indicated for your size, p2—42 (42, 46, 46, 50) sts after completing Row 12.

ROW 13: K1, k1f&b, beg where indicated for your size and inc 1 st in chart as shown, work Row 1 of chart over 40 (40, 44, 44, 48) sts—2 sts inc'd.

ROW 14: Work Row 2 of chart to last 2 sts, ending where indicated for your size, p2.

ROWS 15, 17, 19, 21, AND 23: K1, k1f&b, beg where indicated for your size and inc 1 st in chart as shown, work established chart patt to end—2 sts inc'd each row.

ROWS 16, 18, 20, 22, AND 24: Work in chart patt to last 2 sts, ending where indicated for your size, p2—54 (54, 58, 58, 62) sts after completing Row 24; last chart row completed is Row 12.

For the 3 largest sizes only, work additional rows as foll.

Sizes (42, 46½)" Only

ROW 25: K1, k1f&b, beg where indicated for your size and inc 1 st in chart as shown, work Row 1 of chart over (56, 56) sts—2 sts inc'd.

ROW 26: Work Row 2 of chart to last 2 sts, ending where indicated for your size, p2.

ROWS 27 AND 29: K1, k1f&b, beg where indicated for your size and inc 1 st in chart as shown, work established chart patt to end—2 sts inc'd each row.

ROWS 28 AND 30: Work in chart patt to last 2 sts, ending where indicated for your size, p2—(64, 64) sts after completing Row 30; last chart row completed is Row 6.

Size 50" Only

ROW 25: K1, k1f&b, beg where indicated for your size and inc 1 st in chart as shown, work Row 1 of chart over 60 sts—2 sts inc'd.

ROW 26: Work Row 2 of chart to last 2 sts, ending where indicated for your size, p2.

ROWS 27, 29, 31, 33, AND 35: K1, k1f&b, beg where indicated for your size and inc 1 st in chart as shown, work established chart patt to end—2 sts inc'd each row.

ROWS 28, 30, 32, 34, AND 36: Work in chart patt to last 2 sts, ending where indicated for your size, p2—74 sts after completing Row 36; last chart row completed is Row 12.

All Sizes

Sleeve measures 4½ (4½, 5¼, 5¼, 6¼)" (11.5 [11.5, 13.5, 13.5, 16] cm) from CO—54 (54, 64, 64, 74) sts total.

Body

NOTE: As for left front, maintain 9 sts in established welt patt at shoulder (end of RS rows, beg of WS rows) until these sts are bound off for the neck shaping.

ROW 1: (RS) Use the backward loop method to CO 30 (32, 34, 36, 38) sts for side, work first 8 new sts as [k2, p2] 2 times for lower edge, work rem new sts into established diamond patt, work to last 9 sts, M1P, work in patt to end—85 (87, 99, 101, 113) sts.

ROW 2: (WS) Work in patt to last 8 sts, pm, [k2, p2] 2 times for lower edge.

ROW 3: [K2, p2] 2 times, sl m, work in patt to last 9 sts, M1P, work in patt to end—1 st inc'd at shoulder only.

ROW 4: Work in patt to last 8 sts, sl m, [k2, p2] 2 times.

Rep the last 2 rows 4 (4, 5, 5, 6) more times—90 (92, 105, 107, 120) sts. Discontinue incs at shoulder (end of RS rows) and work even in established patt until body measures 6½ (7, 7½, 8, 8½)" (16.5 [18, 19, 20.5, 21.5] cm) from sts CO at side, ending with a RS row.

Shape Neck

BO 9 sts at beg of next WS row, work in patt to end—81 (83, 96, 98, 111) sts.

DEC ROW: (RS) Work in patt to last 3 sts, k2tog, k1—1 st dec'd.

Work 1 WS row even.

Dec 1 st at neck edge in this manner on the next 5 (6, 7, 8, 9) RS rows, ending with the final RS dec row—75 (76, 88, 89, 101) sts.

Work 4 (4, 6, 6, 8) rows even in patt, ending with a RS row—body measures 2½ (2¾, 3¼, 3½, 4¼)" (6.5 [7, 8.5, 9, 11] cm) from start of neck shaping.

Front Edging

Change to smaller needles. *Purl 1 WS row, knit 2 rows, purl 1 RS row; rep from * once more—body measures 10 (10¾, 11¾, 12½, 13¾)" (25.5 [27.5, 30, 31.5, 35] cm) from sts CO at side; piece measures 14½ (15¼, 17, 17¾, 20)" (37 [38.5, 43, 45, 51] cm) from beg CO.

With WS facing, loosely BO all sts.

BACK

Right Sleeve

CO and work as for left front sleeve—54 (54, 64, 64, 74) sts; sleeve measures 4½ (4½, 5¼, 5¼, 6¼)" (11.5 [11.5, 13.5, 13.5, 16] cm) from CO.

Mark each end of last row completed to indicate end of right sleeve.

Body

NOTE: The beginning and end of the body section are both worked with short-rows (see Glossary) to taper the waist. As for left front, maintain 9 sts in established welt patt at shoulder (beg of RS rows, end of WS rows) until these sts are bound off for the neck shaping, then re-establish the welt patt on these sts after the neck shaping has been completed.

Shape Right Side and Shoulder

ROW 1: (RS) Cont in established patt, work 9 sts, M1P, work in patt to end, pm, use the backward-loop method to CO 30 (32, 34, 36, 38) sts for side—85 (87, 99, 101, 113) sts.

ROW 2: (WS) [P2, k2] 2 times for lower edge, pm, work in patt to end, working rem new CO sts into established diamond patt—22 (24, 26, 28, 30) sts between m.

ROW 3: Work 9 sts in patt, M1P, work in patt to first m, sl m, work 5 sts in patt, wrap the 6th st (see Glossary), turn—86 (88, 100, 102, 114) sts total.

ROW 4: Work in patt to end.

ROW 5: Work 9 sts in patt, M1P, work in patt to first m, sl m, work to wrapped st, work wrap tog with wrapped st, work 5 more sts in patt, wrap the foll st, turn—1 st inc'd at shoulder.

ROW 6: Work in patt to end.

Rep the last 2 rows 1 (2, 2, 2, 3) more time(s)—88 (91, 103, 105, 118) sts total; last wrapped st is the 18 (24, 24, 24, 30)th st after the first m.

NEXT ROW: (RS) Work 9 sts in patt, M1P, work in patt to last 8 sts, working rem wrap tog with wrapped st, [p2, k2] 2 times for lower edge—1 st inc'd at shoulder.

NEXT ROW: (WS) [P2, k2] 2 times, work in patt to end.

Rep the last 2 rows 1 (0, 1, 1, 1) more time—90 (92, 105, 107, 120) sts; piece measures 1¾ (1¾, 2, 2, 2¼)" (4.5 [4.5, 5, 5, 5.5] cm) from end of right sleeve at bustline and about ¾ (1¼, 1¼, 1¼, 1½)" (2 [3.2, 3.2, 3.2, 3.8] cm) less at waist edge (end of RS rows).

Discontinue incs at shoulder and work even in established patt until body measures 6½ (7, 7½, 8, 8½)" (16.5 [18, 19, 20.5, 21.5] cm) from end of right sleeve at bustline, ending with a WS row.

Shape Neck

Cont in patt, BO 5 sts at beg of next RS row, then BO 4 sts at beg of foll RS row—81 (83, 96, 98, 111) sts rem. Work even in patt until neck measures 4 (4, 4, 6, 6)" (10 [10, 10, 15, 15] cm) from first row of neck shaping, ending with a WS row.

Cont in patt and using the backward-loop method, CO 4 sts at beg of next RS row, then CO 5 sts at beg of foll RS row, working new sts in welt patt to match other side of neck—90 (92, 105, 107, 120) sts; neck measures about 4½ (4½, 4½, 6½, 6½)" (11.5 [11.5, 11.5, 16.5, 16.5] cm) from first row of neck shaping.

Shape Left Side and Shoulder

Work even in patt until piece measures 4¾ (5¼, 5½, 6, 6¼)" (12 [13.5, 14, 15, 16] cm) from sts CO at end of neck shaping.

NEXT ROW: (RS) Work 8 sts in patt, p2tog, work in patt to end—1 st dec'd at shoulder.

NEXT ROW: (WS) Work in patt.

Rep the last 2 rows 1 (0, 1, 1, 1) more time—88 (91, 103, 105, 118) sts. Cont to dec at shoulder while working short-rows as foll:

ROW 1: (RS) Work 8 sts in patt, p2tog, work in patt to first m, sl m, work 17 (23, 23, 23, 29) sts, wrap next st, turn—1 st dec'd at shoulder.

ROW 2: Work in patt to end.

ROW 3: Work 8 sts in patt, p2tog, work in patt to 6 sts before previously wrapped st, wrap next st, turn—1 st dec'd at shoulder.

ROW 4: Work in patt to end.

Rep the last 2 rows 1 (2, 2, 2, 3) more times—85 (87, 99, 101, 113) sts rem.

NEXT ROW: (RS) Work 8 sts in patt, p2tog, work in patt to end, working wraps tog with wrapped sts—84 (86, 98, 100, 112) sts rem; last wrapped st is the 6th st after first m for all sizes.

NEXT ROW: (WS) BO 30 (32, 34, 36, 38) sts for side, work in patt to end—54 (54, 64, 64, 74) sts rem; left shoulder measure 6½ (7, 7½, 8, 8½)" (16.5 [18, 19, 20.5, 21.5] cm] from end of neck shaping; back body measures 17½ (18½, 19½, 22½, 23½)" (44.5 [47, 49.5, 57, 59.5] cm] from end of right sleeve at bustline and about 1½ (2½, 2½, 2½, 3)" (3.8 [6.5, 6.5, 6.5, 7.5] cm) less at waist edge between sts CO and BO for sides.

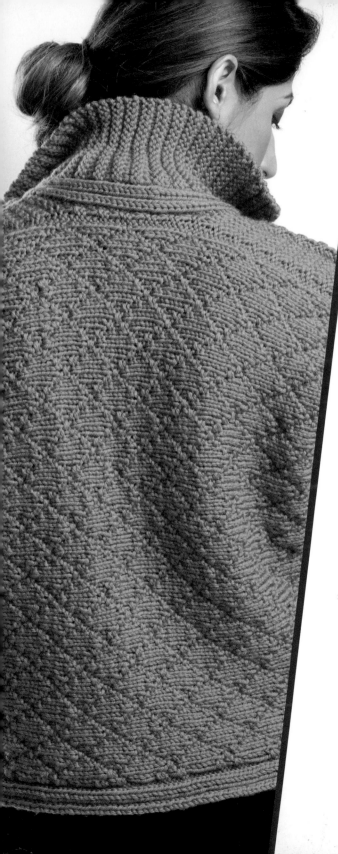

Left Sleeve

Mark each end of last row completed to indicate start of left sleeve.

NEXT ROW: (RS) Work 8 sts in patt, p2tog, work in patt to last 2 sts, ssk—2 sts dec'd.

NEXT ROW: (WS) Work even in patt.

Rep the last 2 rows 11 (11, 14, 14, 17) times—30 (30, 34, 34, 38) sts rem. Change to smaller needles. Work in k2, p2 rib for 8 rows—left sleeve measures 4½ (4½, 5¼, 5¼, 6¼)" (11.5 [11.5, 13.5, 13.5, 16] cm) from marked row; piece measures about 26½ (27½, 30, 33, 36)" (67.5 [70, 76, 84, 91.5] cm) from beg CO.

FINISHING

Weave in loose ends. With yarn threaded on a tapestry needle, sew shoulder and side seams.

Collar

With larger needles, CO 25 sts.

SET-UP ROW: (WS) [K2, p2] 2 times, k2, purl to end.

ROW 1: (RS) P17, [k2, p2] 2 times.

ROW 2: [K2, p2] 2 times, k17.

ROW 3: K15, [p2, k2] 2 times, p2.

ROW 4: [K2, p2] 2 times, k2, p15.

ROW 5: (buttonhole row) P11, BO 3 sts (1 st on right-hand needle after last BO), [p2, k2] 2 times, p2.

ROW 6: [K2, p2] 2 times, k3, use the knitted method to CO 3 sts over gap formed on previous row, knit to end.

ROWS 7 AND 8: Rep Rows 3 and 4.

ROWS 9 AND 10: Rep Rows 1 and 2.

Rep Rows 7–10 until piece measures 18 (18½, 19, 19½, 20)" (45.5 [47, 48.5, 49.5, 51] cm) along k2, p2 edge (end of RS rows), ending with Row 10.

Loosely BO all sts on WS in set-up row patt.

With yarn threaded on a tapestry needle, sew k2, p2 edge of collar to neck opening.

Steam-block to measurements. Sew button to left collar, opposite buttonhole.

Similar to Francesca (page 42) in side-to-side inspiration, this geometric top—designed for winter layering—is a speedy and enjoyable knit. The heavily cabled fabric is inherently stretchy and resilient, while the torso-hugging ribbing gives the piece a slimming fit. The front and back are identical and the shaping is relatively simple, which makes this top a good choice for novice sideways knitters.

TALIA

FINISHED SIZE

About 25 (29, 34, 36½, 38)" (63.5 [73.5, 86.5, 92.5, 96.5] cm) waist circumference.

Sweater shown measures 25" (63.5 cm).

YARN

DK weight (#3 Light).

Shown here: Tahki Dove (44% merino, 44% alpaca, 12% nylon; 163 yd [149 m]/50 g): #008 slate, 5 (6, 7, 7, 8) balls.

NEEDLES

Cuffs, neckband, and waistband: size U.S. 6 (4 mm), 20" (50 cm) circular (cir).

Body and sleeves: size U.S. 8 (5 mm).

Adjust needle size if necessary to obtain the correct gauge.

NOTIONS

Cable needle (cn); markers (m); tapestry needle.

GAUGE

26 sts and 26 rows = 4" (10 cm) in cable patt from chart on larger needles.

stitch guide

K2, P2 RIB (MULTIPLE OF 4 STS + 2)

Row 1: (RS) P2, *k2, p2; rep from *.

Row 2: (WS) K2, *p2, k2; rep from *.

Rep Rows 1 and 2 for pattern.

notes

+ The front and back are worked the same. When each piece is viewed from the RS, the waist edge is at the right-hand side (beginning of RS rows) and the neck edge is at the left-hand side (end of RS rows).

+ During increasing, work the new stitches in reverse stockinette (purl on RS, knit on WS) until there are enough stitches to introduce the cable pattern and still keep 2 reverse stockinette stitches at the selvedge.

+ During decreasing, keep 2 reverse stockinette stitches at each selvedge and convert the cable stitches to reverse stockinette when there are no longer enough stitches to accommodate an entire 2-stitch knit column or a complete 4-stitch cable.

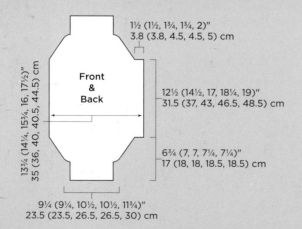

1½ (1½, 1¾, 1¾, 2)"
3.8 (3.8, 4.5, 4.5, 5) cm

Front & Back

13¾ (14¼, 15¾, 16, 17½)"
35 (36, 40, 40.5, 44.5) cm

12½ (14½, 17, 18¼, 19)"
31.5 (37, 43, 46.5, 48.5) cm

6¾ (7, 7, 7¼, 7¼)"
17 (18, 18, 18.5, 18.5) cm

9¼ (9¼, 10½, 10½, 11¾)"
23.5 (23.5, 26.5, 26.5, 30) cm

BACK AND FRONT
(MAKE 2 THE SAME)

First Sleeve

With smaller cir needle, CO 42 (42, 50, 50, 54) sts. Work in k2, p2 rib (see Stitch Guide) until cuff measures 3" (7.5 cm) from CO, ending with a RS row.

Work inc row according to your size as foll.

Sizes 25 (29)" Only

(WS) Work k1f&b (see Glossary) in first st, [k1, k1f&b, k2, k1f&b] 8 times, work k1f&b in last st—60 (60) sts.

Sizes (34, 36½)" Only

(WS) Work k1f&b (see Glossary) in first st, [k2, k1f&b] 16 times, work k1f&b in last st—(68, 68) sts.

Size 38" Only

(WS) Work k1f&b (see Glossary) in first st, [k1, k1f&b, k2, k1f&b] 10 times, k2, work k1f&b in last st—76 sts.

All Sizes

Change to larger needles. Beg with Row 1 (7, 15, 1, 7), work all sts according to Cable chart (see page 56) for 4 rows, ending with Row 4 (10, 2, 4, 10) of chart.

Keeping in patt as established and working new sts into patt (see Notes), inc 1 st each end of needle on the next 10 (11, 11, 12, 12) RS rows, then work 1 WS row even after last inc row—80 (82, 90, 92, 100) sts; piece measures about 6¾ (7, 7, 7¼, 7¼)" (17 [18, 18, 18.5, 18.5] cm) from CO; last row completed is Row 8 (16, 8, 12, 2) of chart.

Body

NEXT ROW: (RS; Row 9 [1, 9, 13, 3] of chart) Using the cable method (see Glossary), CO 10 (10, 12, 12, 14) sts at beg of row (waist edge), work first 4 (4, 6, 6, 8) new CO sts as k2, p2 (2, 4, 4, 6), work rem 86 (88, 96, 98, 106) sts in patt as established—90 (92, 102, 104, 114) sts.

Working sts outside cable patt at waist edge as they appear (knit the knits and purl the purls), work 7 (15, 7, 3, 13) more row(s) to end with Row 16 of chart.

Rep Rows 1–16 of chart 4 (4, 6, 7, 6) times, then work 8 (14, 6, 2, 12) more rows to end with Row 8 (14, 6, 2, 12) of chart.

NEXT ROW: (RS; Row 9 [15, 7, 3, 13] of chart) BO 10 (10, 12, 12, 14) sts, work in patt to end—80 (82, 90, 92, 100) sts; 81 (95, 111, 119, 123) body rows; body measures 12½ (14½, 17, 18¼, 19)" (31.5 [37, 43, 46.5, 48.5] cm) from sts CO at waist edge.

Second Sleeve

Work 1 WS row even. Dec 1 st each end of needle on the next 10 (11, 11, 12, 12) RS rows, ending with the last RS dec row—60 (60, 68, 68, 76) sts rem. Work 4 rows even, ending with a RS row.

Work dec row according to your size as foll.

Sizes 25 (29)" Only

(WS) K2tog, [k1, k2tog, k2, k2tog] 8 times, k2tog—42 (42) sts rem.

Sizes (34, 36½)" Only

(WS) K2tog, [k2, k2tog] 16 times, k2tog—(50, 50) sts rem.

Size 38" Only

(WS) K2tog, [k1, k2tog, k2, k2tog] 10 times, k2, k2tog—54 sts rem.

All Sizes

Change to smaller needle and work in k2, p2 rib for 3" (7.5 cm), ending with a WS row—second sleeve measures about 6¾ (7, 7, 7¼, 7¼)" (17 [18, 18, 18.5, 18.5] cm) from sts BO at end of body; piece measures about 26 (28½, 31, 32¾, 33½)" (66 [72.5, 78.5, 83, 85] cm) overall from CO at start of first sleeve.

With RS facing, BO all sts in rib patt.

FINISHING

Weave in loose ends. Lightly steam-block to measurements.

Neckband

Mark center 12½ (13½, 14½, 15¼, 16)" (31.5 [34.5, 37, 38.5, 40.5] cm) of neck edge on both pieces for neck opening—about 6¾ (7½, 8¼, 8¾, 8¾)" (17 [19, 21, 22, 22] cm) on each side of marked opening.

With yarn threaded on a tapestry needle, sew one shoulder seam from end of sleeve to neck m.

With smaller needle, RS facing, and beg at neck m, pick up and knit 55 (59, 63, 67, 71) sts along neck edge to shoulder seam, place marker (pm), then pick up and knit 55 (59, 63, 67, 71) sts to other neck m—110 (118, 126, 134, 142) sts total.

Purl 1 WS row.

ROW 1: (RS) *P3tog, purl to 3 sts before m, p3tog, slip marker (sl m), p3tog, purl to last 3 sts, p3tog—8 sts dec'd.

ROW 2: (WS) Knit.

ROW 3: K3tog, knit to 3 sts before m, k3tog, sl m, k3tog, knit to last 3 sts, k3tog—8 sts dec'd.

ROW 4: Purl.

Rep Rows 1–3 once more—78 (86, 94, 102, 110) sts rem; 39 (43, 47, 51, 55) sts on each side of m.

With WS facing, BO all sts purlwise.

Sew rem shoulder and neckband seam.

Waistband

Sew side seam seams.

With smaller needle and RS facing, pick up and knit 60 (64, 66, 68, 70) sts along waist edge of front, then 60 (64, 66, 68, 70) sts along waist edge of back—120 (128, 132, 136, 140) sts total. Pm and join for working in rnds.

NEXT RND: K1, *p2, k2; rep from * to last 3 sts, p2, k1.

Rep the last rnd until waistband measures 2½" (6.5 cm) from pick-up rnd.

BO all sts in rib patt.

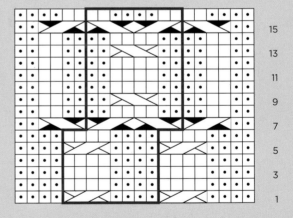

	knit on RS; purl on WS
·	purl on RS; knit on WS
	pattern repeat
⤬	2/2RC: sl 2 sts onto cn and hold in back, k2, k2 from cn
⤬	2/2LC: sl 2 sts onto cn and hold in front, k2, k2 from cn
⤬	2/2RPC: sl 2 sts onto cn and hold in back, k2, p2 from cn
⤬	2/2LPC: sl 2 sts onto cn and hold in front, p2, k2 from cn

Cable

This feminine textured shell was inspired by a cowl-neck top with dropped shoulders that gave the illusion of cap sleeves. That piece was knitted from the bottom up and was shaped with an unbelievably complex sequence of internal short-rows hidden among giant cables. When translated to sideways knitting, however, the shaping becomes a simple matter of increases and decreases placed at the side of the bust and just inside the hem cable. Simply beautiful!

DANI

FINISHED SIZE
36 (40, 43, 47, 52)" (91.5 [101.5, 109, 119.5, 132] cm) bust circumference.

Top shown measures 36" (91.5 cm).

YARN
Sportweight (#2 Fine).

Shown here: Classic Elite Fresco (60% wool, 30% baby alpaca, 10% angora; 164 yd [150 m/50 g]): #5379 purple haze, 5 (7, 7, 8, 10) skeins.

NEEDLES
Size U.S. 6 (4 mm).

Adjust needle size if necessary to obtain the correct gauge.

NOTIONS
Markers (m); cable needle (cn); tapestry needle.

GAUGE
25 sts and 40 rows = 4" (10 cm) in right- and left-slanting broken rib patterns.

25 sts of double garter stitch pattern measure 4" (10 cm) wide.

10 sts of right and left cable patterns measure 1" (2.5 cm) wide.

stitch guide

RIGHT CABLE (WORKED OVER 10 STS)

Set-up row: (WS) K2, p6, k2.

Row 1: (RS) P2, sl 3 sts onto cable needle (cn) and hold in back of work, k3, k3 from cn, p2.

Row 2: K2, p6, k2.

Row 3: P2, k6, p2.

Row 4: Rep Row 2.

Rep Rows 1–4 for pattern; do not rep the set-up row.

LEFT CABLE (WORKED OVER 10 STS)

Set-up row: (WS) K2, p6, k2.

Row 1: (RS) P2, sl 3 sts onto cn and hold in front of work, k3, k3 from cn, p2.

Row 2: (WS) K2, p6, k2.

Row 3: P2, k6, p2.

Row 4: K2, p6, k2.

Rep Rows 1–4 for pattern; do not rep the set-up row.

RIGHT-SLANT BROKEN RIB (MULTIPLE OF 4 STS + 2)

Set-up row: (WS) K1, *p2, k2; rep from * to last st, p1.

Row 1: (RS) *P2, k2; rep from * to last 2 sts, p2.

Row 2: P1, *k2, p2; rep from * to last st, k1.

Row 3: *K2, p2; rep from * to last 2 sts, k2.

Row 4: K1, *p2, k2; rep from * to last st, p1.

Rep Rows 1–4 for pattern.

LEFT-SLANT BROKEN RIB (MULTIPLE OF 4 STS + 2)

Set-up row: (WS) P1, *k2, p2; rep from * to last st, k1.

Row 1: (RS) *P2, k2; rep from * to last 2 sts, p2.

Row 2: K1, *p2, k2; rep from * to last st, p1.

Row 3: *K2, p2; rep from * to last 2 sts, k2.

Row 4: P1, *k2, p2; rep from * to last st, k1.

Rep Rows 1– 4 for pattern.

DOUBLE GARTER STITCH

Row 1: (RS) Purl.

Rows 2 (WS) and 3 (RS): Knit.

Row 4: Purl.

Rep Rows 1–4 for pattern.

notes

+ The front and back are worked the same, from side to side, except the back has left cables at the shoulders and the front has right cables at the shoulders.

+ When each piece is viewed with the RS facing, the shoulder edge is at the right-hand side (beginning of RS rows) and the lower edge is at the left-hand side (end of RS rows).

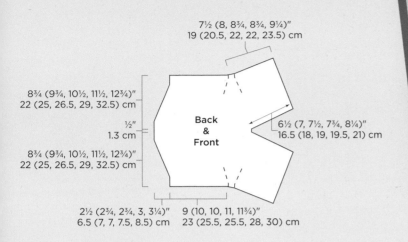

7½ (8, 8¾, 8¾, 9¼)"
19 (20.5, 22, 22, 23.5) cm

8¾ (9¾, 10½, 11½, 12¾)"
22 (25, 26.5, 29, 32.5) cm

½"
1.3 cm

Back
&
Front

6½ (7, 7½, 7¾, 8¼)"
16.5 (18, 19, 19.5, 21) cm

8¾ (9¾, 10½, 11½, 12¾)"
22 (25, 26.5, 29, 32.5) cm

2½ (2¾, 2¾, 3, 3¼)"
6.5 (7, 7, 7.5, 8.5) cm

9 (10, 10, 11, 11¾)"
23 (25.5, 25.5, 28, 30) cm

BACK
Right Side

Using the long-tail method (see Glossary), CO 110 (120, 124, 130, 140) sts.

SET-UP ROW: (WS) Work set-up row of right cable (see Stitch Guide) over 10 sts, place marker (pm), k50 (56, 56, 62, 68), pm, k6, pm, work set-up row of right-slant broken rib (see Stitch Guide) over 34 (38, 42, 42, 46) sts, pm, work set-up row of left cable over 10 sts.

NEXT ROW: (RS) Work Row 1 of left cable over 10 sts, slip marker (sl m), work Row 1 of right-slant broken rib over 34 (38, 42, 42, 46) sts, sl m, purl the next 6 sts for dart worked in Rev St st (purl RS rows; knit WS rows), sl m, work Row 1 of double garter st (see Stitch Guide) over 50 (56, 56, 62, 68) sts, sl m, work Row 1 of right cable over 10 sts.

NEXT ROW: (WS) Cont in established patts, work 1 WS row—piece measures about ½" (1.3 cm).

Shape Right Dart and Lower Edge

The sts in Rev St st between the m are increased to form the bust dart as foll:

DART INC ROW: (RS) Work in patt to first dart m, sl m, M1P (see Glossary), purl to second dart m, M1P, sl m, work in patt to end—2 dart sts inc'd.

Cont in established patts, work 3 rows even, working new sts in Rev St st, and beg and ending with a WS row.

Rep the last 4 rows 1 (2, 2, 3, 4) more time(s), then work inc row once more, ending with RS Row 3 of double garter patt—116 (128, 132, 140, 152) sts total; 12 (14, 14, 16, 18) Rev St dart sts; piece measures 1½ (1¾, 1¾, 2¼, 2½)" (3.8 [4.5, 4.5, 5.5, 6.5] cm) from CO.

NOTE: Measure all lengths straight up along a single column of sts; do not measure along diagonal shaping lines.

Cont dart incs while inc at lower edge as foll:

Work 3 rows even in established patts, beg and ending with a WS row.

DART AND LOWER EDGE INC ROW: (RS) Work in patt to first dart m, sl m, M1P, purl to second dart m, M1P, sl m, work in patt to last 10 sts, M1 (see Glossary) or M1P as needed to maintain patt, sl m, work in patt to end—3 sts inc'd total: 2 dart sts, 1 double garter st.

Rep the last 4 rows 3 (4, 5, 5, 6) more times, then work 1 WS row even, working new sts into their respective patts, ending with WS Row 4 of double garter patt—128 (143, 150, 158, 173) sts; 20 (24, 26, 28, 32) Rev St dart sts; 54 (61, 62, 68, 75) double garter sts between dart section and lower edge cable; piece measures 3¼ (3¾, 4¼, 4¾, 5½)" (8.5 [9.5, 11, 12, 14] cm) from CO.

NEXT ROW: (RS) Work 10 cable sts, work established right-slant broken rib patt to last 10 sts, removing m on each side of dart as you come to them and working former dart and double garter sts into broken rib patt, sl m, work 10 cable sts.

NEXT ROW: (WS) Work even in established patts.

LOWER EDGE INC ROW: (RS) Work in patt to last 10 sts, M1 or M1P as needed to maintain broken rib patt, work 10 cable sts—1 st inc'd.

Cont in established patts, work 3 rows even, beg and ending with a WS row.

Rep the last 4 rows 9 (10, 10, 11, 12) more times, then work lower edge inc row once more, ending with a RS row—139 (155, 162, 171, 187) sts total; 119 (135, 142, 151, 167) broken rib sts between cables; piece measures 7½ (8½, 9, 9¾, 11)" (19 [21.5, 23, 25, 28] cm) from CO.

Work 13 (13, 15, 17, 17) rows even in patt, ending with a WS row—piece measures 8¾ (9¾, 10½, 11½, 12¾)" (22 [25, 26.5, 29, 32.5] cm) from CO.

Make a note of the last broken rib row worked so you can start the pattern with the correct row on the other side of the neck shaping.

Shape Neck

ROW 1: (RS) BO 44 (48, 50, 52, 56) sts for right back neck edge, purl to last

10 sts, work 10 sts in established cable patt—95 (107, 112, 119, 131) sts rem.

ROW 2: (WS) Work 10 sts in cable patt, knit to end.

ROW 3: Purl to last 10 sts, work 10 sts in cable patt.

ROW 4: (WS) Work 10 sts in cable patt, knit to end, use the backward-loop method (see Glossary) to CO 44 (48, 52, 56) sts for left back neck edge—139 (155, 162, 171, 187) sts; Rev St st neck shaping section measures about ½" (1.3 cm) high.

Shape Left Dart and Lower Edge

NOTE: The right cable pattern continues as established; the lower edge and the left cable pattern resume on the second shoulder. The broken rib pattern switches to the left-slant version for the second half of the back so the rib patts will mirror each other and create a chevron effect on each side of the Rev St st center strip. If you ended the right-slant broken rib with Row 4 before the neck shaping, begin the left-slant broken rib with Row 3; if you ended the right-slant pattern with Row 2, begin the left-slant pattern with Row 1. The number of broken rib stitches will not be a multiple of 4 stitches plus 2, so start the pattern row as given in the Stitch Guide, then work any leftover stitches into the established patt.

NEXT ROW: (RS) Work left cable over first 10 sts (use the same-number pattern row as will be worked for the

right cable at the end of this row), pm, work Row 1 or Row 3 of left-slant broken rib to last 10 sts, sl m, work 10 sts in cable patt.

Cont patts as established, work 11 (11, 13, 15, 15) rows even, beg and ending with a WS row—piece measures about 1¼ (1¼, 1½, 1¾, 1¾)" (3.2 [3.2, 3.8, 4.5, 4.5] cm) from end of neck shaping.

LOWER EDGE DEC ROW: (RS) Work in patt to last 12 sts, work 2 sts tog as p2tog or k2tog as necessary to maintain broken rib patt, sl m, work 10 sts in cable patt—1 st dec'd.

Cont in established patts, work 3 rows even, beg and ending with a WS row.

Rep the last 4 rows 9 (10, 10, 11, 12) more times, then work the lower edge dec row once more, then work 1 WS row even in patt—128 (143, 150, 158, 173) sts rem; 108 (123, 130, 138, 153) left-slant broken rib sts between cables; piece measures about 5½ (6, 6¼, 6¾, 7¼)" [14 [15, 16, 17, 18.5] cm) from end of neck shaping.

Establish Rev St st dart sts and double garter sts on next row as foll:

NEXT ROW: (RS) Work 10 cable sts, work 32 (38, 42, 42, 46) sts in established broken rib, pm, p20 (24, 26, 28, 32) for Rev St st dart sts, pm, p56 (61, 62, 68, 75) for Row 1 of double garter patt, sl m, work 10 cable sts.

NEXT ROW: (WS) Work 1 row even in established patts.

Cont lower edge decs while dec for dart as foll:

DART AND LOWER EDGE DEC ROW: (RS) Work in patt to m before first dart m, sl m, ssp (see Glossary), purl to 2 sts before second dart m, p2tog, sl m, work in patt to 2 sts before lower edge cable m, work 2 sts tog as p2tog or k2tog as necessary to maintain broken rib patt, sl m, work 10 sts in cable patt—3 sts dec'd total: 2 dart sts, 1 double garter st.

NEXT 3 ROWS: Work 3 rows even in established patts, beg and ending with a WS row.

Rep the last 4 rows 3 (4, 5, 5, 6) more times, ending with a WS row—116 (128, 132, 140, 152) sts rem; 12 (14, 14, 16, 18) Rev St dart sts; piece measures 7¼ (8, 8¾, 9¼, 10¼)" (18.5 [20.5, 22, 23.5, 26] cm) from end of neck shaping.

Dec for dart only as foll:

DART DEC ROW: (RS) Work in patt to m before first dart m, sl m, ssp, purl to 2 sts before second dart m, p2tog, sl m, work in patt to end—2 dart sts dec'd.

Work 3 rows even in established patts, beg and ending with a WS row.

Rep the last 4 rows 1 (2, 2, 3, 4) more time(s), then work dec row once more—110 (120, 124, 130, 140) sts; 6 dart sts rem; piece measures 8¼ (9¼, 10, 11, 12¼)" (21 [23.5, 25.5, 28, 31] cm) from end of neck shaping.

Work 4 rows even in established patts, ending with a RS Row 3 of double garter patt—piece measures 8¾ (9¾, 10½, 11½, 12¾)" (22 [25, 26.5, 29, 32.5] cm) from end of neck shaping and 18 (20, 21½, 23½, 26)" (45.5 [51, 54.5, 59.5, 66] cm) from initial CO.

BO all sts loosely.

FRONT

Using the long-tail method, CO 110 (120, 124, 130, 140) sts.

SET-UP ROW: (WS) Work set-up row of right cable over 10 sts, pm, k50 (56, 56, 62, 68), pm, k6, pm, work set-up row of right-slant broken rib over 34 (38, 42, 42, 46) sts, pm, work set-up row of right cable over 10 sts (see Notes).

Complete as for back, using the right cable patt at both the lower edge and shoulders throughougt.

FINISHING

Weave in loose ends. Lightly steam-block pieces to measurements.

With yarn threaded on a tapestry needle, sew front to back at left shoulder.

Neckband

With RS facing and beg at right back shoulder, pick up and knit 45 (49, 52, 54, 58) sts evenly spaced along right back neck to center of V, 45 (49, 52, 54, 58) sts along left back neck to shoulder seam, 45 (49, 52, 54, 58) sts along left front neck to center of V, and 45 (49, 52, 54, 58) sts along right front neck to shoulder—180 (196, 208, 216, 232) sts total. [Knit 1 WS row, purl 2 rows, knit 1 RS row] 2 times, knit 1 WS row.

With RS facing, loosely BO all sts pwise.

Sew neckband and right shoulder seam.

Sew side seams along lower edge cable and double garter patts, leaving Rev St st dart sts, broken rib sts, and shoulder cable sts free for armhole openings.

This slim-fitting sweater is reminiscent of styles from the 1950s and 1960s but is updated with long sleeves and goblet cuffs. Triangular garter panels angle from armhole to center waist to give a body-conscious fit with an artistic flair. This texture is echoed in the reverse stockinette-stitch short-row shoulder shaping. To keep the integrity of the pattern, be sure to work the wraps together with the wrapped stitches so that the wraps fall to the back of the work.

LYNETTE

FINISHED SIZE

36½ (39½, 43½, 47½, 51½)" (92.5 [100.5, 110.5, 120.5, 131] cm) bust circumference, including 2½" (6.5 cm) front band.

Sweater shown measures 36½" (92.5 cm).

YARN

Sportweight (#2 Fine).

Shown here: Rowan Felted Tweed (50% merino, 25% alpaca, 25% viscose; 191 yd [175 m]/50 g): #152 watery (aqua), 8 (9, 9, 10, 11) balls.

NEEDLES

Body and ribbings: size U.S. 6 (4 mm).

Bell cuffs and collar: size U.S. 3 (3.25 mm).

Adjust needle size if necessary to obtain the correct gauge.

NOTIONS

Markers (m); removable markers or waste yarn; stitch holders; tapestry needle; five ¾" (2 cm) buttons.

GAUGE

23 sts and 30 rows = 4" (10 cm) in St st on larger needles with single strand of yarn.

23 sts and 40 rows = 4" (10 cm) in garter st on larger needles with single strand of yarn.

22 sts and 46 rows = 4" (10 cm) in garter st on smaller needles with yarn doubled.

notes

+ The body and sleeves are worked in two mirror-image halves that start at the sleeve opening and work toward the center of the body. Each sleeve begins with a garter-stitch cuff worked separately with a doubled strand of yarn, then stitches for the sleeve are picked up along one edge of the cuff.

+ The back ribbed waistband is picked up and worked down from the lower edge. The front bands are picked up along the lower and center front edges and worked in one piece with mitered corners. These ribbings are not shown on the schematic and will add about 2½" (6.5 cm) to the finished body length.

+ The collar (also not shown on the schematic) is worked separately in garter stitch with a doubled strand of yarn and is sewn to the body during finishing.

+ The schematic for this project does not show the garment parts oriented in the direction of the knitting.

LEFT HALF

Cuff

With smaller needles and yarn doubled, CO 18 sts. Work short-rows (see Glossary) as foll:

ROW 1 (RS)–ROW 8 (WS): Knit.

ROW 9: K15, wrap next st, turn work.

ROWS 10, 12, AND 14: Knit.

ROW 11: K10, wrap next st, turn.

ROW 13: K5, wrap next st, turn.

ROW 15: Knit across all sts, working wraps tog with wrapped sts.

ROW 16: Knit.

Rep these 16 rows 9 (9, 10, 10, 11) more times—160 (160, 176, 176, 192) rows total; piece measures 14 (14, 15¼, 15¼, 16¾)" (35.5 [35.5, 38.5, 38.5, 42.5] cm) from CO along wider selvedge (beg of RS rows, end of WS rows) and 8¾ (8¾, 9½, 9½, 10½)" (22 [22, 24, 24, 26.5] cm) from CO along narrower selvedge (end of RS rows, beg of WS rows).

With RS facing, BO all sts kwise.

Sleeve

With larger needles, single strand of yarn, and RS facing, pick up and knit 43 (47, 51, 55, 59) sts evenly spaced along narrower selvedge of cuff. Work even in St st until piece measures 4" (10 cm) from pick-up row, ending with a WS row.

NOTE: If adjusting sleeve length, work more or fewer inches at this point and be sure to make the same change on the right half sleeve.

INC ROW: (RS) K2, M1 (see Glossary), knit to last 2 sts, M1, k2—2 sts inc'd.

Work 3 rows even in St st. Rep the last 4 rows 21 (22, 23, 24, 25) more times, ending with a WS row—87 (93, 99, 105, 111) sts. BO 8 (9, 10, 11, 12) sts at beg of next 2 rows—71 (75, 79,

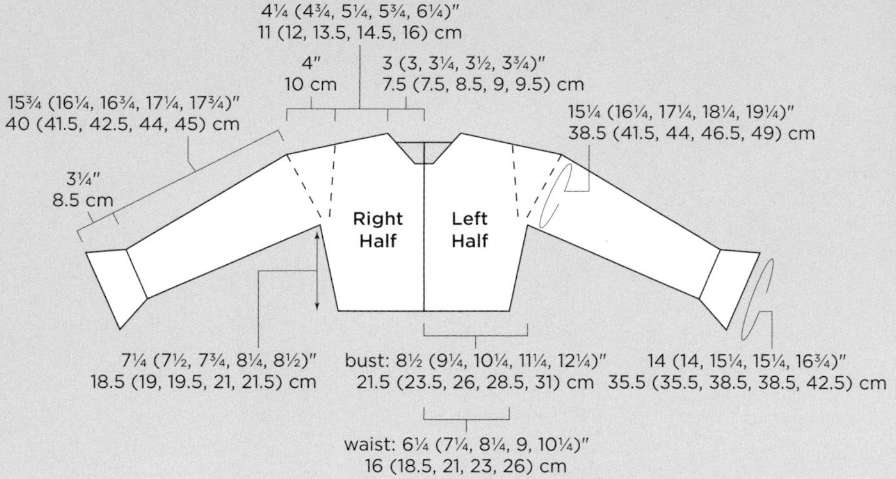

4¼ (4¾, 5¼, 5¾, 6¼)"
11 (12, 13.5, 14.5, 16) cm

4"
10 cm

3 (3, 3¼, 3½, 3¾)"
7.5 (7.5, 8.5, 9, 9.5) cm

15¾ (16¼, 16¾, 17¼, 17¾)"
40 (41.5, 42.5, 44, 45) cm

15¼ (16¼, 17¼, 18¼, 19¼)"
38.5 (41.5, 44, 46.5, 49) cm

3¼"
8.5 cm

Right Half   Left Half

7¼ (7½, 7¾, 8¼, 8½)"
18.5 (19, 19.5, 21, 21.5) cm

bust: 8½ (9¼, 10¼, 11¼, 12¼)"
21.5 (23.5, 26, 28.5, 31) cm

14 (14, 15¼, 15¼, 16¾)"
35.5 (35.5, 38.5, 38.5, 42.5) cm

waist: 6¼ (7¼, 8¼, 9, 10¼)"
16 (18.5, 21, 23, 26) cm

83, 87) sts rem; piece measures 15¾ (16¼, 16¾, 17¼, 17¾)" (40 [41.5, 42.5, 44, 45] cm) from pick-up row and about 3¼" (8.5 cm) longer to lower edge of cuff.

Mark each end of last row completed to indicate end of sleeve.

Shape Cap

Work short-rows in wedges of alternating Rev St st (purl on RS rows, knit on WS rows) and St st as foll:

ROW 1: (RS; beg Rev St st) K10, purl to last 10 sts, wrap next st, turn work.

ROW 2: (WS) Knit to last 10 sts, wrap next st, turn.

ROWS 3 AND 4: Work in Rev St st to last 15 sts, wrap next st, turn.

ROWS 5 AND 6: Work in Rev St st to last 20 sts, wrap next st, turn.

ROW 7: (RS; beg St st) Knit to last 5 sts, working wraps tog with wrapped sts.

ROW 8: Purl to last 5 sts, working rem wraps tog with wrapped sts.

ROWS 9 AND 10: Work in St st to last 10 sts, wrap next st, turn.

ROWS 11 AND 12: Work across all sts in St st, working wraps tog with wrapped sts.

ROWS 13-18: Rep Rows 1–6.

ROWS 19-24: Rep Rows 7–12.

ROWS 25-30: Rep Rows 1–6—piece measures 4" (10 cm, from marked row at end of sleeve measured straight up at center along shoulder line and ½" (1.3 cm) from marked sleeve row at selvedges.

Cut yarn and place sts on holder.

Back Side Panel

With larger needles, CO 41 (43, 45, 47, 49) sts. Knit 3 rows, beg and ending with a RS row.

Work short-rows to narrow the piece from armhole to waist as foll:

ROW 1: (WS) K35 (34, 33, 32, 31), wrap next st, turn.

ROWS 2 AND 4: (RS) Knit to end.

ROW 3: K25 (24, 23, 22, 21), wrap next st, turn.

ROW 5: Knit to end, working wraps tog with wrapped sts.

Knit 5 (7, 9, 11, 13) rows even across all sts, beg and ending with a RS row—piece measures about 1¼ (1½, 1¾, 2, 2¼)" (3.2 [3.8, 4.5, 5, 5.5] cm) from CO at armhole edge (end of RS rows) and about ¾ (1, 1¼, 1½, 1¾)" (2 [2.5, 3.2, 3.8, 4.5] cm) at lower edge (beg of RS rows).

Cut yarn and place sts on holder.

Front Side Panel

With larger needles, CO 41 (43, 45, 47, 49) sts. Knit 2 rows.

Work short-rows to narrow the piece from armhole to waist as foll:

ROW 1: (RS) K35 (34, 33, 32, 31), wrap next st, turn.

ROWS 2 AND 4: (WS) Knit to end.

ROW 3: K25 (24, 23, 22, 21), wrap next st, turn.

ROW 5: Knit to end, working wraps tog with wrapped sts.

Knit 6 (8, 10, 12, 14) rows even across all sts, ending with a RS row—piece measures about 1¼ (1½, 1¾, 2, 2¼)" (3.2 [3.8, 4.5, 5, 5.5] cm) from CO at armhole edge (beg of RS rows) and about ¾ (1, 1¼, 1½, 1¾)" (2 [2.5, 3.2, 3.8, 4.5] cm) at lower edge (end of RS rows).

Do not cut yarn; leave sts on needle.

Join Sleeve and Side Panels

With WS facing, k41 (43, 45, 47, 49) front panel sts, place marker (pm), purl first 33 (35, 37, 39, 41) sleeve sts, pm, p5 center sleeve sts, pm, purl last 33 (35, 37, 39, 41) sleeve sts, k41 (43, 45, 47, 49) back panel sts—153 (161, 169, 177, 185) sts total.

Body

NOTE: As you work the shoulder increases, the garter st of the side panels will gradually transition to St st.

ROW 1: (RS) Knit to end of side panel sts, slip marker (sl m), knit to next m, M1, sl m, k5, sl m, M1, knit to end of sleeve sts, sl m, knit across side panel sts to end—155 (163, 171, 179, 187) sts.

ROW 2: (WS) Knit to 2 sts before side panel m, p2, sl m, purl across all sleeve sts to next side panel m, sl m, p2, knit to end—2 garter sts changed to St st in each side panel.

ROW 3: Knit.

ROW 4: Knit to last 2 garter sts of previous WS row, p2, purl to next garter st section, p2, knit to end—2 garter sts changed to St st in each side panel.

ROW 5: (RS; inc row) Knit to m before center sts, M1, sl m, k5, sl m, M1, knit to end—2 sts inc'd.

ROW 6: Rep Row 4—2 garter sts changed to St st in each side panel.

Rep Rows 3–6 only 6 (7, 8, 9, 10) more times, ending with a WS row—169 (179, 189, 199, 209) sts; 11 (9, 7, 5, 3) garter sts rem at each end of row; St st fabric measures 4¼ (4¾, 5¼, 5¾, 6¼)" (11 [12, 13.5, 14.5, 16] cm) from joining row measured straight up along center of 5-st section at shoulder (do not measure along diagonal shaping); garter fabric measures 3¾ (4½, 5¼, 5¾, 6½)" (9.5 [11.5, 13.5, 14.5, 16.5] cm) from sts CO for side panels at each end of row.

NOTE: While shaping back neck, cont to transition rem garter sts to St st at a rate of 2 sts every WS row as established until 1 garter st rem, then work all sts in St st to end.

NEXT ROW: (RS) Removing markers as you come to them, k79 (84, 89, 94, 99), k2tog, k1, place rem 87 (92, 97, 102, 107) sts on holder to work later for front—81 (86, 91, 96, 101) back sts rem.

Back Neck

Work 1 WS row even in patt, transitioning 2 garter sts to St st.

DEC ROW: (RS) Work in patt to last 3 sts, k2tog, k1—1 st dec'd.

Work 1 WS row even, cont garter st transition as necessary for your size. Rep the last 2 rows 2 (2, 2, 3, 3) more times—78 (83, 88, 92, 97) sts rem; back neck depth (width of sts removed by neck shaping) measures about ¾ (¾, ¾, 1, 1)" (2 [2, 2, 2.5, 2.5] cm).

Work 14 (14, 16, 16, 18) rows even, cont garter st transition as necessary for your size and ending with a WS row—back neck measures 3 (3, 3¼, 3½, 3¾)" (7.5 [7.5, 8.5, 9, 9.5] cm) from where front sts were placed on holder; all sts have been converted to St st; piece measures 7¼ (7¾, 8½, 9¼, 10)" (18.5 [19.5, 21.5, 23.5, 25.5] cm) from joining row at base of armhole (bust line), 8½

(9¼, 10¼, 11¼, 12¼)" (21.5 [23.5, 26, 28.5, 31] cm) from sts CO for side panels at bust line, and 6¼ (7¼, 8¼, 9, 10¼)" (16 [18.5, 21, 23, 26] cm) from sts CO for side panels at waist edge (beg of RS rows).

Loosely BO all sts.

Front Neck

NOTE: As for back neck, cont to transition rem garter sts to St st at a rate of 2 sts every WS row.

Return 87 (92, 97, 102, 107) held front sts to larger needles and rejoin yarn with RS facing, ready to work a RS row.

NEXT ROW: (RS) BO 5 sts, knit to end, removing m as you come to them—82 (87, 92, 97, 102) sts rem.

Work 1 WS row even in patt, transitioning 2 garter sts to St st.

DEC ROW: (RS) K1, ssk, knit to end—1 st dec'd.

Work 1 WS row even, cont garter st transition as necessary for your size.

Rep the last 2 rows 7 (7, 8, 8, 9) more times—74 (79, 83, 88, 92) sts rem; front neck depth (width of sts removed by neck shaping) measures about 2¼ (2¼, 2½, 2½, 2¾)" (5.5 [5.5, 6.5, 6.5, 7] cm). Work 4 (4, 4, 6, 6) rows even—front neck measures 3 (3, 3¼, 3½, 3¾)" (7.5 [7.5, 8.5, 9, 9.5] cm) from where front and back divided, and the same from base of armhole and along lower edge as for back.

Loosely BO all sts.

RIGHT HALF

Sleeve

CO and work as for left half to end of sleeve cap shaping—71 (75, 79, 83, 87) sts rem; piece measures 4" (10 cm) from marked row at end of sleeve measured straight up at center along shoulder line and ½" (1.3 cm) from marked sleeve row at selvedges.

Cut yarn and place sts on holder.

Side Panels

CO and work front side panel same as for left half back side panel, ending with a RS row—41 (43, 45, 47, 49) sts; piece measures about 1¼ (1½, 1¾, 2, 2¼)" (3.2 [3.8, 4.5, 5, 5.5] cm) from CO at armhole edge (end of RS rows) and about ¾ (1, 1¼, 1½, 1¾)" (2 [2.5, 3.2, 3.8, 4.5] cm) at lower edge (beg of RS rows).

Cut yarn and place sts on holder.

CO and work back side panel same as for left half front side panel, ending with a RS row—41 (43, 45, 47, 49) sts; piece measures same as other side panel.

Do not cut yarn; leave sts on needle.

Join Sleeve and Side Panels

With WS facing, k41 (43, 45, 47, 49) back panel sts, pm, purl first 33 (35, 37, 39, 41) sleeve sts, pm, p5 center sleeve sts, pm, purl last 33 (35, 37, 39, 41) sleeve sts, k41 (43, 45, 47, 49) front panel sts—153 (161, 169, 177, 185) sts total.

Body

Work as for left half, ending with a WS row—169 (179, 189, 199, 209) sts; 11 (9, 7, 5, 3) garter sts rem at each end of row; St st fabric measures 4¼ (4¾, 5¼, 5¾, 6¼)" (11 [12, 13.5, 14.5, 16] cm) from joining row measured straight up along center of 5-st section at shoulder and garter fabric measures 3¾ (4½, 5¼, 5¾, 6½)" (9.5 [11.5, 13.5, 14.5, 16.5] cm) from sts CO for side panels at each end of row.

Front Neck

NOTE: As for left half, cont to transition rem garter sts to St st as established until 1 garter st rem, then work all sts in St st to end.

NEXT ROW: (RS) Removing markers as you come to them, k87 (92, 97, 102, 107), place rem 82 (87, 92, 97, 102) sts on holder to work later for back—87 (92, 97, 102, 107) front sts rem.

NEXT ROW: (WS) BO 5 sts, work in patt to end, transitioning 2 garter sts to St st—82 (87, 92, 97, 102) sts.

DEC ROW: (RS) Work in patt to last 3 sts, k2tog, k1—1 st dec'd.

Work 1 WS row even, cont garter st transition as necessary for your size.

Rep the last 2 rows 7 (7, 8, 8, 9) more times—74 (79, 83, 88, 92) sts rem; front neck depth (width of sts removed by neck shaping) measures about 2¼ (2¼, 2½, 2½, 2¾)" (5.5 [5.5, 6.5, 6.5, 7] cm). Work 4 (4, 4, 6, 6) rows even—front neck measures 3 (3, 3¼, 3½, 3¾)" (7.5 [7.5, 8.5, 9, 9.5] cm) from where back sts were placed on holder; all sts have been converted to St st; piece measures 7¼ (7¾, 8½, 9¼, 10)" (18.5 [19.5, 21.5, 23.5, 25.5] cm) from joining row at base of armhole (bust line), 8½ (9¼, 10¼, 11¼, 12¼)" (21.5 [23.5, 26, 28.5, 31] cm) from sts CO for side panels at bust line, and 6¼ (7¼, 8¼, 9, 10¼)" (16 [18.5, 21, 23, 26] cm) from sts CO for side panels at waist edge (beg of RS rows).

Loosely BO all sts.

Back Neck

NOTE: As for front neck, cont to transition rem garter sts to St st as established until 1 garter st rem, then work all sts in St st to end.

Return 82 (87, 92, 97, 102) held back sts to needle and rejoin yarn with RS facing, ready to work a RS row.

DEC ROW: (RS) K1, ssk, work in patt to end—1 st dec'd.

Work 1 WS row even, cont garter st transition as necessary for your size. Rep the last 2 rows 3 (3, 3, 4, 4) more times—78 (83, 88, 92, 97) sts rem; back neck depth (width of sts removed by neck shaping) measures about ¾ (¾, ¾, 1, 1)" (2 [2, 2, 2.5, 2.5] cm). Work 14 (14, 16, 16, 18) rows even—back neck measures 3 (3, 3¼, 3½, 3¾)" (7.5 [7.5, 8.5, 9, 9.5] cm) from where front and back divided, piece measures the same from base of armhole and along lower edge as for left half after back neck shaping.

Loosely BO all sts.

FINISHING

Weave in loose ends. Block to measurements. With yarn threaded on a tapestry needle, sew center back seam.

Lower Back Ribbing

With larger needles and RS facing, pick up and knit 66 (70, 74, 78, 82) sts evenly spaced along lower back edge.

ROW 1: (WS) *K2, p2; rep from * to last 2 sts, k2.

ROW 2: (RS) *P2, k2; rep from * to last 2 sts, p2.

Rep these 2 rows 8 more times, then work WS Row 1 once more—19 rows completed; ribbing measures 2½" (6.5 cm) from pick-up row.

Loosely BO all sts in patt.

Right Front Band

With larger needles, RS facing, and beg at side edge of right front, pick up and knit 30 (34, 38, 42, 46) sts evenly spaced along lower right front edge, pm, 1 st in corner, pm, then 60 (64, 68, 72, 76) sts along center front edge—91

(99, 107, 115, 123) sts total.

ROW 1: (WS) *K2, p2; rep from * to corner st, sl m, p1 (corner st), **p2, k2; rep from ** to last st, p2.

ROW 2: (RS) Work in established rib to m, inc 1 st using either M1 or M1P (see Glossary) to maintain k2, p2 rib patt, sl m, k1 (corner st), sl m, inc 1 st using either M1 or M1P to maintain rib patt, work in established rib to end—2 sts inc'd.

ROW 3: (WS) Work sts as they appear (knit the knits and purl the purls), working new sts into k2, p2 rib patt.

Rep the last 2 rows 3 more times, ending with a WS row—99 (107, 115, 123, 131) sts; 64 (68, 72, 76, 80) front sts between corner st and neck edge.

BUTTONHOLE ROW: (RS) Work in established rib to m, M1 or M1P to maintain patt, sl m, k1 (corner st), sl m, M1 or M1P to maintain patt, work 8 (10, 8, 10, 8) sts in patt, *k2tog, [yo] 2 times, ssk, work 8 (8, 10, 10, 12) sts in rib patt; rep from * 3 more times, k2tog, [yo] 2 times, ssk, work 4 (6, 4, 6, 4) sts in rib patt— 5 buttonholes; 2 sts inc'd.

NEXT ROW: (WS) *Work in rib patt to first double yo, work [k1, p1] in double yo; rep from * 4 more times,

work in patt to m, sl m, p1 (corner st), sl m, work in patt to end.

Rep Rows 2 and 3 from before the buttonhole 4 more times, ending with a WS row—109 (117, 125, 133, 141) sts; 19 rows completed; ribbing measures 2½" (6.5 cm) from pick-up row.

Loosely BO all sts in patt.

Left Front Band

With larger needles, RS facing, and beg at neck edge of left front, pick up and knit 60 (64, 68, 72, 76) sts evenly spaced along center front edge, pm, 1 st in corner, pm, then 30 (34, 38, 42, 46) sts along lower left front edge—91 (99, 107, 115, 123) sts total.

ROW 1: (WS) P2, *k2, p2; rep from * to corner st, sl m, p1 (corner st), **p2, k2; rep from ** to end.

ROW 2: (RS) Work in established rib to m, inc 1 st using either M1 or M1P to maintain k2, p2 rib patt, sl m, k1 (corner st), sl m, inc 1 st using either M1 or M1P to maintain rib patt, work in established rib to end—2 sts inc'd.

ROW 3: (WS) Work sts as they appear (knit the knits and purl the purls), working new sts into k2, p2 rib patt.

Rep the last 2 rows 8 more times,

ending with a WS row—109 (117, 125, 133, 141) sts; 19 rows completed; ribbing measures 2½" (6.5 cm) from pick-up row.

Loosely BO all sts in patt.

Collar

With smaller needles and yarn doubled, CO 18 sts. Knit 10 rows.

INC ROW: (RS) Knit to last 2 sts, k1f&b, k1—1 st inc'd at neck edge.

Knit 7 rows even, beg and ending with a WS row.

Rep the last 8 rows 8 (8, 8, 9, 9) more times—27 (27, 27, 28, 28) sts; piece measures about 7¼ (7¼, 7¼, 7¾, 7¾)" (18.5 [18.5, 18.5, 19.5, 19.5] cm) from CO. Work even in garter st (knit every row) until selvedge of collar reaches from BO edge of front rib band to center back seam.

Place removable marker at each end of last row to mark center of collar.

Work an equal number of garter rows for the other side of the collar, ending with a WS row.

DEC ROW: (RS) Knit to last 3 sts, k2tog, k1—1 st dec'd.

Knit 7 rows even. Rep the last 8 rows 8 (8, 8, 9, 9) more times—18 sts rem. Knit 10 rows.

Loosely BO all sts.

With yarn threaded on a tapestry needle, sew shaped edge of collar to neckline so that ends of collar are aligned with BO edges of front bands and center of collar is aligned with back seam. Sew side, sleeve, and cuff seams.

Lightly steam-press. Sew buttons to left front, opposite buttonholes.

two
MOSTLY
SIDEWAYS

Every designer has limitations, and I've found that my own have led me to find creative ways to punch up the volume on my designs. For example, I frequently turn an existing traditional piece on its side, which often changes a ho-hum shape into a fresh, vibrant design. This allows me the opportunity to pick up stitches along an edge and work in a perpendicular direction. Although the process is essentially the same as sideways knitting, the picked-up stitches often add another interesting design element. In three of the four designs in this chapter, the picked-up stitches do just that.

When I began thinking about sideways work, I set about finding a way to bring a bit of lace into the collection. Dominique (page 78) stands alone in her lacy triumph, but stays true to the sideways concept—the sleeves are knitted sideways, then joined with another panel at the back. I used the same construction technique for Merielle (page 86), but with cables instead of lace. The geometric shape creates a great drape while internal increases ensure a flattering fit.

I came up with Gemma (page 94) completely by accident while knitting on a different design late at night—the time when mistakes are most often made. Luckily, my mistake gave me an idea and this little cape burst out of an effort to save a flawed piece of knitting. Let this be a reminder not to be too quick to rip out your next mistake—you never know where it may lead.

For the guys, I present Erik (page 100), a jacket with all the earmarks of a tailored coat, minus the shoulder pads. The nicely rounded sleeve caps give a custom-made look without unnecessary bulk. Despite the textured moss stitch and cable details, I think the fully lined collar is what really stands out, or—in this case—stands up in this design.

Inspired by the ever-popular triangular lace shawl, I set out to create a similar look in a sideways-knitted jacket. It turns out that if you knit a triangular shawl and stop increasing when it's close to the desired sleeve length, a suitable shoulder angle is magically produced. Knit another one, and you have two halves of something quite wearable. All that's left is to knit a panel to connect the two halves and add a skirt, and you have a stunning piece for layering!

DOMINIQUE

FINISHED SIZE

About 25 (29, 35, 40, 44)" (63.5 [73.5, 89, 101.5, 112] cm) waist circumference, with front edgings touching at center.

Jacket shown measures 25" (63.5 cm) at waist.

YARN

Worsted weight (#4 Medium).

Shown here: Classic Elite Yarns Portland Tweed (50% wool, 25% alpaca, 25% viscose; 120 yd [110 m]/50 g): #5054 barely there lilac, 6 (8, 9, 11, 12) balls.

NEEDLES

Sleeves, upper body, and upper skirt: size U.S. 7 (4.5 mm): 24" or 32" (60 or 80 cm) circular (cir).

Lower skirt: sizes U.S. 8 and 9 (5 and 5.5 mm): 24" or 32" (60 or 80 cm) cir.

Adjust needle size if necessary to obtain the correct gauge.

NOTIONS

Tapestry needle; removable markers or waste yarn.

GAUGE

17 sts and 27½ rows = 4" (10 cm) in lace pattern from Chart A or B on smallest needle, after blocking.

19–21 sts of Chart D for center back insert measure 4" (10 cm) wide on smallest needle, after blocking.

16 sts and 21½ rows = 4" (10 cm) in feather and fan pattern on largest needle, after blocking.

stitch guide

FEATHER AND FAN PATTERN (MULTIPLE OF 18 STS + 4)

Row 1: (RS) K2, [k2tog] 3 times, *[yo, k1] 6 times, [k2tog] 6 times; rep from * to last 14 sts, [yo, k1] 6 times, [k2tog] 3 times, k2.

Row 2: (WS) K2, purl to last 2 sts, k2.

Rows 3, 4, and 5: Knit.

Row 6: Rep Row 2.

Rep Rows 1–6 for pattern.

Note: Some versions of this pattern use both right- and left-slanting decreases (k2tog and ssk), but this project deliberately uses k2tog decreases throughout.

notes

+ Each half of the upper body is worked like a modified triangular shawl from the armhole opening toward the shoulder. A center back panel joins the two halves, then stitches for the skirt are picked up and worked downward from the lower edge of the body, gradually increasing the needle size to flare the skirt.

+ The schematic shows the measurements after blocking.

+ The first time you work Chart B there will only be enough stitches to work each red pattern repeat box once. After completing the chart the first time, the stitch count will have increased by 40 stitches total, 20 stitches in each half. This will allow you to work each 10-stitch red outlined box 3 times when you next work Chart B and 5 times in any subsequent repeat of Chart B, if required by your size.

+ Chart D for the center back insert begins with 19 cast-on stitches, increases to 21 stitches after completing Row 1, then decreases back to 19 stitches after completing Row 5.

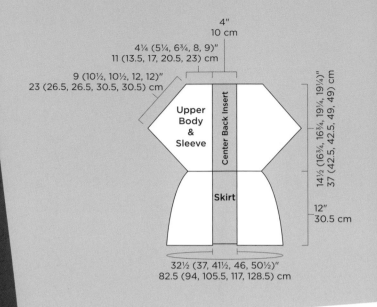

4"
10 cm

4¼ (5¼, 6¾, 8, 9)"
11 (13.5, 17, 20.5, 23) cm

9 (10½, 10½, 12, 12)"
23 (26.5, 26.5, 30.5, 30.5) cm

14½ (16¾, 16¾, 19¼, 19¼)"
37 (42.5, 42.5, 49, 49) cm

Upper Body & Sleeve

Center Back Insert

Skirt

12"
30.5 cm

32½ (37, 41½, 46, 50½)"
82.5 (94, 105.5, 117, 128.5) cm

SLEEVE AND UPPER BODY (MAKE 2)

With smallest needle, CO 5 sts. Knit 2 rows, ending with a WS row.

NEXT ROW: (RS) K1, k1f&b (see Glossary), k1, k1f&b, k1—7 sts.

NEXT ROW: (WS) K2, p3, k2.

Work Rows 1–28 of Chart A (see page 82)—63 sts.

Establish patt from Row 1 of Chart B (see page 82) as foll: Work 32 sts of the Right Half chart, inc them to 34 sts and working the red patt rep box only once, then work the 31 sts of the Left Half chart, inc them to 33 sts and working the red patt rep box only once—67 sts.

Work Rows 2–20 of Chart B—103 sts. Work Rows 1–20 of Chart B 0 (1, 1, 1, 1) more time(s) (see Notes), then work Rows 1–10 of Chart B 1 (0, 0, 1, 1) time(s)—123 (143, 143, 163, 163) sts; 62 (72, 72, 82, 82) rows total from CO; piece measures about 9 (10½, 10½, 12, 12)" (23 [26.5, 26.5, 30.5, 30.5] cm) along each selvedge and straight up along the center st, after blocking.

Shape Shoulder

NOTE: Chart C (see page 84) is worked even without any increases inside the garter st selvedges or adjacent to the center stitch. This creates straight selvedges along each side that form the lower edges of the upper body and also creates a "dart" effect in the center that hugs the shoulder attractively. The patt rep changes to 18 rows in Chart C.

Mark the center stitch and each end of last row completed to indicate start of the shoulder.

Work Rows 1–18 of Chart C (see page 84) 1 (1, 2, 2, 3) time(s), then work Row 1 through Row 9 (17, 9, 17, 9) once more—27 (35, 45, 53, 63) rows total from Chart C.

Knit 3 rows, beg and ending with a WS row—shoulder measures about 4¼ (5¼, 6¾, 8, 9])" (11 [13.5, 17, 20.5, 23] cm) from marked row at start of shoulder shaping, after blocking.

Loosely BO all sts.

Make a second sleeve and upper body piece the same as the first.

CENTER BACK INSERT

Block sleeve and upper body pieces to measurements.

With smallest needle, CO 19 sts. Rep Rows 1–10 of Chart D (see Notes; also see page 84) until piece measures 4" (10 cm) wide and 14½ (16¾, 16¾, 19¼, 19¼)" (37 [42.5, 42.5, 49, 49] cm) from CO after blocking, ending with a WS row.

NOTE: Temporarily transfer sts to a holding string to block if necessary.

Loosely BO all sts.

Mark the center of the BO row on each upper body and sleeve piece to indicate the shoulder line.

With yarn threaded on a tapestry needle, sew one selvedge of the center back insert to the BO edge of an upper body and sleeve piece between its shoulder line and selvedge (lower edge of body). Sew rem selvedge of center back insert between the shoulder line and selvedge of the other upper body and sleeve piece, making sure that you have a right and left sleeve with an opening down the center front.

SKIRT

With smallest needle, RS facing, and beg at the left front edge, pick up and knit 26 (30, 35, 39, 44) sts along lower edge of left front, 26 (31, 35, 40, 44) sts across left back, 26 sts across center back insert, 26 (31, 35, 40, 44) sts across right back, and 26 (30, 35, 39, 44) sts across right front—130 (148, 166, 184, 202) sts total.

NOTE: The pick-up row joins the bases of the sleeve openings.

Knit 3 rows, beg and ending with a WS row—2 garter ridges. Rep Rows 1–6 of feather and fan patt (see Stitch Guide) until piece measures about 3" (7.5 cm) from pick-up row. Change to

medium-size needle and cont in patt for 3″ (7.5 cm) more. Change to largest needle and cont in patt until piece measures 10″ (25.5 cm) from pick-up row, ending with a RS row. Knit 6 rows, ending with a RS row.

With WS facing, loosely BO all sts as if to knit—4 garter ridges.

FINISHING

Weave in loose ends. Carefully steam-press and block the skirt to measure 12″ (30.5 cm) long from pick-up row and 32½ (37, 41½, 46, 50½)″ (82.5 [94, 105.5, 117, 128.5] cm) along BO edge.

Front Edging

With smallest needles, RS facing, and beg at lower right front corner of skirt, pick up and knit 253 (273, 273, 293, 293) sts evenly spaced along front opening, ending at lower left front corner of skirt.

NEXT ROW: (WS) K2, purl to last 2 sts, k2.

ROWS 1, 3, AND 5: (RS) K2, *yo, k3, sl 2 sts as if to k2tog, k1, pass 2 sl sts over, k3, yo, k1; rep from * to last st, k1.

ROWS 2, 4, AND 6: (WS) K2, purl to last 2 sts, k2.

ROW 7: K2, *yo, k9, yo, k1; rep from * to last st, k1—303 (327, 327, 351, 351) sts.

ROW 8: Knit.

With WS facing, loosely BO all sts as if to knit—edging will measure about 2″ (5 cm) from pick-up row, after blocking.

With yarn threaded on a tapestry needle, work a few strong tacking stitches at the base of each sleeve opening, just above the pick-up row of the skirt.

Steam-press and block again, opening the lace pattern of the front edging and coaxing each [yo, k1, yo] in Row 9 of edging into a gentle point.

Chart A

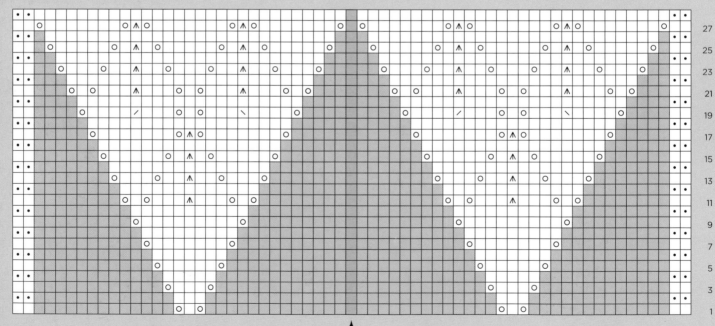

center st

Legend

□	k on RS; p on WS
·	p on RS; k on WS
O	yo
/	k2tog
\	ssk
ʌ	sl 2 as if to k2tog, k1, pass 2 sl sts over
⋌	k3tog
▨	no stitch
▦	center stitch: k on RS; p on WS
ʌ (shaded)	center stitch: sl 2 as if to k2tog, k1, pass 2 sl sts over
▭	pattern repeat

Chart B, Right Half

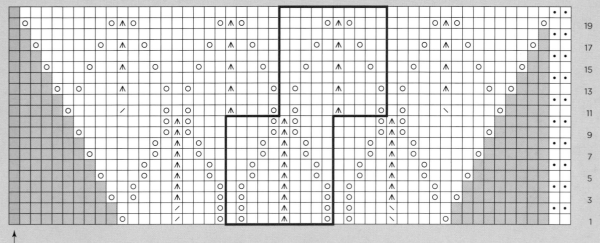

center st

Chart B, Left Half

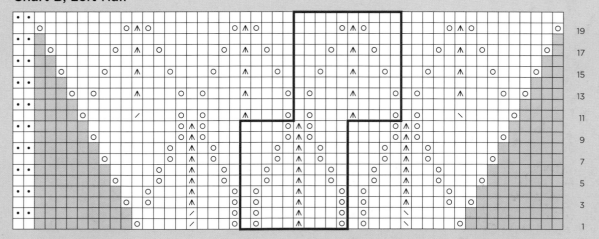

	k on RS; p on WS		ssk		no stitch
•	p on RS; k on WS	⋏	sl 2 as if to k2tog, k1, pass 2 sl sts over		center stitch: k on RS; p on WS
O	yo	⋌	k3tog	⋏	center stitch: sl 2 as if to k2tog, k1, pass 2 sl sts over
/	k2tog				pattern repeat

Chart C

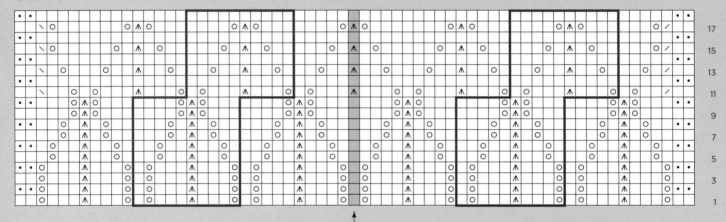

center st

Chart D

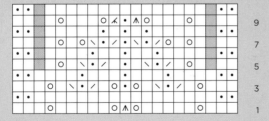

This design was literally turned 90 degrees on its side. I had planned a bottom-up dolman, but as I pinned together the first incarnation for a fitting, I accidentally folded one of the fronts along the center—what was once a hem became a wrist and the cable ran up the arm rather than up the front. Instead of a hip-length dolman, I had a cropped jacket with a triangular silhouette. Internal shaping produces the great angle of the body; a shawl collar adds warm style.

MERIELLE

FINISHED SIZE

About 39 (42, 46, 50, 52)" (99 [106.5, 117, 127, 132] cm) lower edge circumference, with front bands overlapped 1" (2.5 cm).

Sweater shown measures 46" (117 cm).

YARN

Worsted weight (#4 Medium).

Shown here: Berroco Peruvia (100% wool; 174 yd [160 m]/100 g): #7148 boysenberry, 6 (7, 7, 8, 8) skeins.

NEEDLES

Size U.S. 8 (5 mm).

Adjust needle size if necessary to obtain the correct gauge.

NOTIONS

Cable needle (cn); markers (m); waste yarn for stitch holders; tapestry needle; removable markers or waste yarn; three ¾" (2 cm) buttons.

GAUGE

19 sts and 25 rows = 4" (10 cm) in St st; 38 sts of shoulder cable patt from chart measure 6" (15 cm) wide.

16 sts and 36 rows (6 patt reps) of horseshoe cable patt measure 2" (5 cm) wide and 5¼" (13.5 cm) long.

stitch guide

HORSESHOE CABLE (WORKED OVER 16 STS)

Row 1: (RS) P2, sl 3 sts onto cable needle (cn) and hold in back, k3, k3 from cn, sl 3 sts onto cn and hold in back, k3, k3 from cn, p2.

Rows 2 and 4: (WS) K2, p12, k2.

Rows 3 and 5: P2, k12, p2.

Row 6: Rep Row 2.

Rep Rows 1–6 for pattern.

notes

+ The piece is worked in two mirror-image halves that start at the sleeve opening and are worked toward the center of the body.

+ Each sleeve begins with a cabled cuff band worked separately, then stitches for the sleeve are picked up along one edge of the band.

+ The center back cable panel, lower body cabled band, and collar are worked separately and sewn to the body halves during finishing.

+ The schematic for this project does not show the garment parts oriented in the direction of the knitting.

LEFT HALF

Cuff

CO 16 sts.

SET-UP ROW: (WS) K2, p12, k2.

Rep Rows 1–6 of horseshoe cable patt (see Stitch Guide) 15 (16, 17, 18, 19) times, then work Row 1 once more—92 (98, 104, 110, 116) rows total; piece measures 13½ (14¼, 15¼, 16, 17)" (34.5 [36, 38.5, 40.5, 43] cm) from CO. BO all sts.

Sleeve

Hold cuff band with RS facing and selvedge at end of RS rows running horizontally across the top, then pick up and knit 64 (68, 72, 76, 80) sts evenly spaced along the upper edge of the band (about 7 sts for every 10 rows).

SET-UP ROW: (WS) P13 (15, 17, 19, 21), place marker (pm), [k2, p2] 9 times, k2, pm, p13 (15, 17, 19, 21).

Work the sts as they appear (knit the knits, and purl the purls) for 0 (0, 2, 2, 4) rows, ending with a WS row.

NEXT ROW: (RS) Knit to 2 sts before m, M1 (see Glossary), k2, slip marker (sl m), work Row 1 of Shoulder Cable chart (see page 91) over center 38 sts, sl m, k2, M1, knit to end—66 (70, 74, 78, 82) sts.

NEXT 3 ROWS: Work even in patt, working sts outside cable panel in St st and beg and ending with a WS row.

INC ROW: (RS) Knit to 2 sts before m, M1, k2, sl m, work cable patt over 38 sts, sl m, k2, M1, knit to end—2 sts inc'd.

Working new sts in St st, cont in established patt and rep the last 4 rows 13 (12, 11, 10, 9) more times, then work 1 WS row even—94 (96, 98, 100, 102) sts; 59 (55, 53, 49, 47) rows completed; piece measures about

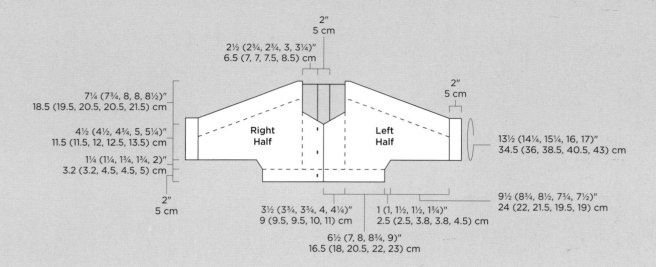

2″
5 cm

2½ (2¾, 2¾, 3, 3¼)″
6.5 (7, 7, 7.5, 8.5) cm

7¼ (7¾, 8, 8, 8½)″
18.5 (19.5, 20.5, 20.5, 21.5) cm

4½ (4½, 4¾, 5, 5¼)″
11.5 (11.5, 12, 12.5, 13.5) cm

1¼ (1¼, 1¾, 1¾, 2)″
3.2 (3.2, 4.5, 4.5, 5) cm

2″
5 cm

Right Half

Left Half

2″
5 cm

13½ (14¼, 15¼, 16, 17)″
34.5 (36, 38.5, 40.5, 43) cm

3½ (3¾, 3¾, 4, 4¼)″
9 (9.5, 9.5, 10, 11) cm

1 (1, 1½, 1½, 1¾)″
2.5 (2.5, 3.8, 3.8, 4.5) cm

9½ (8¾, 8½, 7¾, 7½)″
24 (22, 21.5, 19.5, 19) cm

6½ (7, 8, 8¾, 9)″
16.5 (18, 20.5, 22, 23) cm

9½ (8¾, 8½, 7¾, 7½)″ (24 [22, 21.5, 19.5, 19] cm) from pick-up row measured straight up along a single column of sts (do not measure along diagonal shaping line) and 2″ (5 cm) longer from lower edge of cuff band.

NOTE: The larger sizes have increasingly wider bodies, so their sleeves are shorter to prevent the overall "wingspan" of the garment from becoming too wide.

Mark each end of last row completed to indicate end of sleeve.

Body

Cont to inc 1 st on each side of cable panel every 4th row as established while shaping sides with short-rows and CO sts as foll:

ROW 1: (RS) Use the backward-loop method (see Glossary) to CO 6 (6, 8, 8, 10) sts at beg of row, knit across new

sts, work in patt to end—100 (102, 106, 108, 112) sts.

ROW 2: (WS) Use the backward-loop method to CO 6 (6, 8, 8, 10) sts at beg of row, purl across new sts, work in patt to last 6 (6, 8, 8, 10) sts, p1, wrap next st, turn—106 (108, 114, 116, 122) sts.

ROW 3: (RS, inc row) Knit to 2 sts before cable panel, M1, k2, sl m, work 38 cable sts, sl m, k2, M1, knit to last 6 (6, 8, 8, 10) sts, k1, wrap next st, turn—2 sts inc'd; wrapped st at each side is 2nd st of new CO sts.

ROWS 4 AND 6: Work in patt to previously wrapped st, work wrap tog with wrapped st, p1, wrap next st, turn.

ROW 5: Work in patt to previously wrapped st, work wrap tog with wrapped st, k1, wrap next st, turn.

ROW 7: (inc row) Knit to 2 sts before cable panel, M1, k2, sl m, work 38

cable sts, sl m, k2, M1, work in patt to previously wrapped st, work wrap tog with wrapped st, k1, wrap next st, turn—2 sts inc'd.

Rep the last 4 rows 0 (0, 0, 0, 1) more time(s), then work Rows 4 and 5 only 0 (0, 1, 1, 0) time(s), ending with a RS row—110 (112, 118, 120, 128) sts; last wrapped st at each side is the selvedge st; piece measures 1 (1, 1½, 1½, 1¾)″ (2.5 [2.5, 3.8, 3.8, 4.5] cm) from end of sleeve.

NOTE: From here, cont to inc 1 st on each side of cable panel every 4th row as established; for sizes 39″, 42″, and 52″, which ended with inc Row 7, you will need to work 3 rows even before the next RS inc row; for sizes 46″ and 50″, which ended with Row 5, the next RS row will be an inc row.

Cont in patt and working wraps tog with wrapped sts as you come to them, use the backward-loop method to CO

16 sts at beg of the next 2 rows, inc 0 (0, 1, 1, 0) st on each side of the cable panel as established in the second of these rows, and ending with a RS row—142 (144, 152, 154, 160) sts.

NEXT ROW: (WS) K2, p12, k2, pm, work in patt to last 16 sts, pm, k2, p12, k2.

Working 16 sts at each end of row in horseshoe cable patt, work 0 (0, 2, 2, 0) rows even.

Cont in patts, inc 1 st on each side of center cable panel on the next RS row, then every 4th row 9 (10, 11, 12, 13) more times, ending with the final RS inc row—162 (166, 176, 180, 188) sts: 16 sts in horseshoe cable at each side, 38 center shoulder cable sts, 46 (48, 53, 55, 59) sts in each St st section.

Work 7 rows even in patts, beg and ending with a WS row—piece measures about 6½ (7, 8, 8¾, 9)" (16.5 [18, 20.5, 22, 23] cm) from sts CO for horseshoe cable bands at lower edge.

Dividing Row

NEXT ROW: (RS) Work 78 (80, 85, 87, 91) back sts in patt, place rem 84 (86, 91, 93, 97) sts on waste yarn to work later for front.

Back Neck

NOTE: Cont shoulder cable as charted until sts fall into a k2, p2 rib patt arrangement, then work the cable sts in k2, p2 rib to end.

Working 78 (80, 85, 87, 91) back sts only and cont horseshoe cable at lower edge as established, work 14 (16, 16, 18, 20) rows even, ending with a RS row—back neck measures 2½ (2¾, 2¾, 3, 3¼)" (6.5 [7, 7, 7.5, 8.5] cm) from dividing row; piece measures about 9 (9¾, 10¾, 11¾, 12¼)" (23 [25, 27.5, 30, 31] cm) from sts CO for horseshoe cable band at lower edge and 21½ (21½, 22¾, 23, 23½)" (54.5 [54.5, 58, 58.5, 59.5] cm) from beg overall, including 2" (5 cm) cuff band.

With WS facing, BO all sts.

Front

Return 84 (86, 91, 93, 97) held sts to needle and rejoin yarn with RS facing, ready to work a RS row.

ROW 1: (RS) BO 31 (32, 33, 34, 35) sts, knit if necessary for your size until there are 1 (2, 2, 3, 2) st(s) on right-hand needle after BO, [p2, k2] 9 (9, 10, 10, 11) times, work 16 horseshoe cable sts as established—53 (54, 58, 59, 62) sts rem.

ROW 2: (WS) Work the sts as they appear.

ROW 3: Ssk, work the sts as they appear to the last 16 sts, work 16 sts of horseshoe cable—1 st dec'd.

ROW 4: Work sts as they appear.

Rep the last 2 rows 9 (10, 10, 10, 10) more times—43 (43, 47, 48, 51) sts rem; front measures 3½ (3¾, 3¾, 3¾, 3¾)" (9 [9.5, 9.5, 9.5, 9.5] cm) from dividing row.

⬜	knit on RS; purl on WS
⊡	purl on RS; knit on WS
◹	2/1RPC: sl 1 st onto cn and hold in back, k2, p1 from cn
◸	2/1LPC: sl 2 sts onto cn and hold in front, p1, k2 from cn
⬿	2/2RC: sl 2 sts onto cn and hold in back, k2, k2 from cn
⤫	2/2LC: sl 2 sts onto cn and hold in front, k2, k2 from cn
◤	2/2RPC: sl 2 sts onto cn and hold in back, k2, p2 from cn
◣	2/2LPC: sl 2 sts onto cn and hold in front, p2, k2 from cn

Shoulder Cable

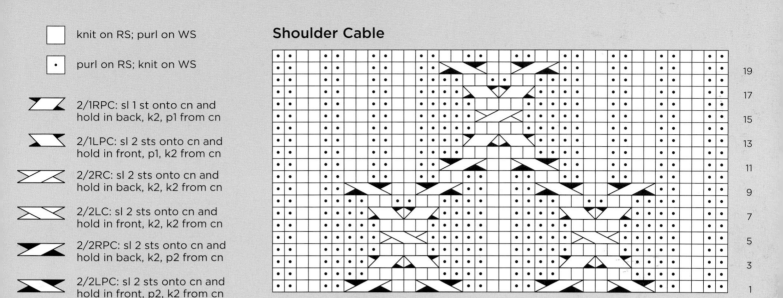

Work even if necessary for your size until front measures 3½ (3¾, 3¾, 4, 4¼)" (9 [9.5, 9.5, 10, 11] cm) from dividing row, ending with a WS row.

BO all sts in rib patt.

RIGHT HALF

Work cuff and sleeve as for left half—94 (96, 98, 100, 102) sts; piece measures 9½ (8¾, 8½, 7¾, 7½)" (24 [22, 21.5, 19.5, 19] cm) from pick-up row and 2" (5 cm) longer from lower edge of cuff band.

Body

Work body as for left half until incs on each side of shoulder cable have been

completed, ending with the final RS inc row—162 (166, 176, 180, 188) sts; 16 horseshoe cable sts at each side, 38 center shoulder cable sts, 46 (48, 53, 55, 59) sts in each St st section.

Work 6 rows even in patts, ending with a RS row—piece measures about 6½ (7, 8, 8¾, 9)" (16.5 [18, 20.5, 22, 23] cm) from sts CO for horseshoe cable bands at lower edge.

Dividing Row

With WS facing, work 78 (80, 85, 87, 91) back sts in patt, place rem 84 (86, 91, 93, 97) sts on waste yarn to work later for front.

Back Neck

NOTE: As for left half, cont shoulder cable until sts are arranged as for a k2, p2 rib, then work these sts in rib patt to the end.

Working 78 (80, 85, 87, 91) back sts only and cont horseshoe cable at lower edge as established, work 15 (17, 17, 19, 21) rows even, ending with a RS row—back neck measures 2½ (2¾, 2¾, 3, 3¼)" (6.5 [7, 7, 7.5, 8.5] cm) from dividing row; piece measures 9 (9¾, 10¾, 11¾, 12¼)" (23 [25, 27.5, 30, 31] cm) from sts CO for horseshoe cable band at lower edge and 21½ (21½, 22¾, 23, 23½)" (54.5 [54.5, 58, 58.5, 59.5] cm) from beg overall, including 2" (5 cm) cuff band.

With WS facing, BO all sts.

Front

Return 84 (86, 91, 93, 97) held sts to needle and rejoin yarn with WS facing, ready to work a WS row.

ROW 1: (WS) BO 31 (32, 33, 34, 35) sts, purl if necessary for your size until there are 1 (2, 2, 3, 2) st(s) on right-hand needle after BO, [k2, p2] 9 (9, 10, 10, 11) times, work 16 horseshoe cable sts as established—53 (54, 58, 59, 62) sts rem.

ROW 2: (RS) Work in patt to last 2 sts, k2tog—1 st dec'd.

ROW 3: Work sts as they appear.

Rep the last 2 rows 4 (5, 5, 5, 5) more times, ending with a WS row—48 (48, 52, 53, 56) sts.

BUTTONHOLE ROW: (RS) Work first 6 sts of horseshoe cable, k2tog, yo, ssk, work last 6 sts of horseshoe cable, work 6 (6, 7, 7, 8) sts in rib patt, k2tog, yo, ssk, work 12 (12, 13, 13, 14) sts in rib patt, k2tog, yo, ssk, work 4 (4, 6, 7, 8) sts in rib patt, k2tog—44 (44, 48, 49, 52) sts rem.

NEXT ROW: (WS) Work in rib patt, working [k1, p1] in each of the 3 yo in buttonhole row—47 (47, 51, 52, 55) sts.

Rep Rows 2 and 3 from before buttonhole row 4 more times—43 (43, 47, 48, 51) sts rem; front measures 3½ (3¾, 3¾, 3¾, 3¾)" (9 [9.5, 9.5, 9.5, 9.5] cm) from dividing row.

Work even if necessary for your size until front measures 3½ (3¾, 3¾, 4, 4¼)" (9 [9.5, 9.5, 10, 11] cm) from dividing row, ending with a WS row.

BO all sts in rib patt.

CENTER BACK PANEL

CO 16 sts.

SET-UP ROW: (WS) K2, p12, k2.

Rep Rows 1–6 of horseshoe cable patt 16 (16, 18, 18, 19) times, then work Row 1 once more—98 (98, 110, 110, 116) rows total; piece measures 14¼ (14¼, 16, 16, 17)" (36 [36, 40.5, 40.5, 43] cm) from CO.

BO all sts.

FINISHING

Weave in loose ends. Lightly steam-block each piece, being careful not to flatten cables.

With yarn threaded on a tapestry needle, sew center back panel to back edge of each body half, easing to fit. Sew sleeve and side seams.

Collar

CO 5 sts, placing a marker on each side of center st.

INC ROW: Knit to m, yo, sl m, k1, sl m, yo, knit to end—2 sts inc'd.

Knit 3 rows even.

Rep the last 4 rows 6 (6, 7, 7, 8) more times, then work inc row once more—21 (21, 23, 23, 25) sts; piece measures about 2½ (2½, 3, 3, 3¼)" (6.5 [6.5, 7.5, 7.5, 8.5] cm) from CO, measured straight up in center.

Work even in garter st (knit every row) until selvedge of collar reaches from BO edge of front rib band to center back neck.

Place removable marker at each end of last row to mark center of collar. Work even for an equal number of garter rows for the other side of the collar.

DEC ROW: Knit to 3 sts before m, k3tog, yo, sl m, k1, sl m, yo, k3tog through back loops (tbl), knit to end—2 sts dec'd.

Knit 3 rows even.

Rep the last 4 rows 6 (6, 7, 7, 8) more times—7 sts rem for all sizes.

NEXT ROW: K3tog, yo, sl m, k1, sl m, yo, k3tog tbl—5 sts rem.

BO all sts.

Sew collar to neckline, matching marked row in center of back neck to middle of center back insert. Sew buttons to left front, opposite buttonholes.

This cape evolved from a chunky scarf that I put down mid-row many times only to pick up and work in the wrong direction. I realized that my "mistakes" could be ideal shaping for the body section of a cape. For the yoke, stitches are picked up around the non-cable edge, and the shoulders and neck are shaped with decreases. The collar is then picked up and knitted with a cable pattern at each center front (not visible in photographs) and, as for Erik (page 100), lined for extra stiffness and drama.

GEMMA

FINISHED SIZE

About 61¾ (67, 72, 77¼, 82½)" (157 [170, 183, 196, 209.5] cm) circumference at lower edge and 39½ (42¾, 46, 49½, 52¾)" (100.5 [108.5, 117, 125.5, 134] cm) circumference at base of yoke, with 1¼" (3.2 cm) front bands overlapped.

Capelet shown measures 39½" (100.5 cm) at base of yoke.

YARN

Worsted weight (#4 Medium).

Shown here: Rowan Felted Tweed Aran (50% merino, 25% alpaca, 25% viscose; 95 yd [87 m]/50 g): #729 soot (charcoal), 9 (10, 11, 12, 14) balls.

NEEDLES

Size U.S. 9 (5.5 mm): 24" or 32" (60 or 80 cm) circular (cir).

Adjust needle size if necessary to obtain the correct gauge.

NOTIONS

Markers (m); cable needle (cn); tapestry needle; three 1¼" (3.2 cm) buttons.

GAUGE

16 sts and 21½ rows = 4" (10 cm) in St st.

24 sts of cable patt from chart measure about 3¾" (9.5 cm) wide, after blocking.

notes

+ The body of the capelet is worked sideways using short-rows, beginning at the right front edge, continuing around the body, and ending at the left front edge.

+ To prevent the sideways-knitted fabric from stretching too much, the body begins with a firm cast-on and ends with a sturdy bind-off. The front bands are picked up and worked out from the ends of the body, instead of being worked from live stitches, which helps prevent the front edges from stretching over time with wear.

+ To choose a size, measure the circumference of your upper body just below the collarbone and around the outside your upper arms. Select the base-of-yoke measurement that will provide the desired amount of positive ease compared to this body measurement.

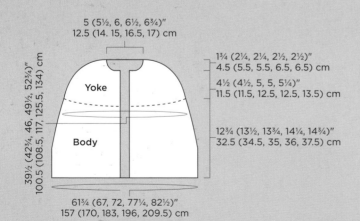

5 (5½, 6, 6½, 6¾)"
12.5 (14. 15, 16.5, 17) cm

Yoke

Body

39½ (42¾, 46, 49½, 52¾)" cm
100.5 (108.5, 117, 125.5, 134) cm

1¾ (2¼, 2¼, 2½, 2½)"
4.5 (5.5, 5.5, 6.5, 6.5) cm

4½ (4½, 5, 5, 5¼)"
11.5 (11.5, 12.5, 12.5, 13.5) cm

12¾ (13½, 13¾, 14¼, 14¾)"
32.5 (34.5, 35, 36, 37.5) cm

61¾ (67, 72, 77¼, 82½)"
157 (170, 183, 196, 209.5) cm

BODY

CO 60 (62, 64, 66, 68) sts.

SET-UP ROW: (WS) K2, p3, k4, p6, k4, p3, k2, place marker (pm), purl to end—24 sts in marked section for cable patt; 36 (38, 40, 42, 44) St sts.

ROW 1: (RS) Work in St st to m, slip marker (sl m), work Row 1 of Cable chart (see page 98) to end.

ROWS 2 AND 3: Work 2 rows even, cont cable patt as established and working rem sts in St st.

Work short-rows (see Glossary) on Rows 4–13 as foll:

ROW 4: (WS) Work cable patt to marker (m), sl m, wrap next st, turn.

ROW 5: (RS) Sl m, work cable patt to end.

ROW 6: Work cable patt to m, sl m, work wrap tog with previous wrapped st, p7 (7, 7, 7, 8), wrap next st, turn.

ROW 7: Knit to m, sl m, work cable patt to end.

ROW 8: Work cable patt to m, purl to wrapped st, work wrap tog with previous wrapped st, p7, wrap next st, turn.

ROW 9: Knit to m, sl m, work cable patt to end.

ROWS 10–13: Rep Rows 8 and 9 two more times.

Working last wrap tog with wrapped st as you come to it, resume working across all sts as foll:

ROWS 14–31: Work 18 rows even in patt, ending with a RS row.

Cont cable patt as established, rep Rows 4–31 (do not include Rows 1–3 in rep) 10 (11, 12, 13, 14) more times, then work Rows 4–16 once more, ending with Row 4 (16, 12, 8, 4) of cable patt—325 (353, 381, 409, 437) rows total at lower edge (end of RS rows), including set-up row; 205 (223, 241, 259, 277) rows total at yoke edge (beg of RS rows), including set-up row; piece measures about 60½ (65¾, 70¾, 76, 81¼)" (153.5 [167, 179.5, 193,

206.5] cm) from CO along cabled lower edge and 38¼ (41½, 44¾, 48¼, 51½)" (97 [105.5, 113.5, 122.5, 131] cm) along yoke edge.

BO all sts.

YOKE

With RS facing and beg at right front edge, pick up and knit 137 (149, 161, 173, 185) sts evenly spaced along yoke edge.

ROWS 1 (WS) AND 2 (RS): Purl.

ROW 3: Knit.

ROW 4: K2, *k2tog, k4; rep from * to last 3 sts, k2tog, k1—114 (124, 134, 144, 154) sts rem.

ROWS 5 AND 6: Purl.

ROWS 7 AND 8: Knit.

ROWS 9–11: Rep Rows 5–7 once more, ending with a WS row—yoke measures about 2" (5 cm) from pick-up row.

Shape Shoulders

SET-UP ROW: (RS) K28 (31, 33, 36, 38) right front sts, pm, k58 (62, 68, 72, 78) back sts, pm, k28 (31, 33, 36, 38) left front sts.

Purl 1 WS row.

DEC ROW: (RS) [Knit to 4 sts before m, k3tog, k1, sl m, k1, sssk (see Glossary)] 2 times, knit to end—8 sts dec'd.

Purl 1 WS row.

Rep the last 2 rows 5 (5, 6, 6, 7) more times—66 (76, 78, 88, 90) sts; 34 (38, 40, 44, 46) back sts; 16 (19, 19, 22, 22) sts each front; yoke measures about 4½ (4½, 5, 5, 5¼)" (11.5 [11.5, 12.5, 12.5, 13.5] cm) from pick-up row.

Shape Neck

ROWS 1 AND 2: BO 10 (11, 12, 13, 14) sts at beg of next 2 rows and *at the same time* work double decs on each side of both shoulder m as established on the RS row of these 2 rows—38 (46, 46, 54, 54) sts rem; 30 (34, 36, 40, 42) back sts; 4 (6, 5, 7, 6) sts each front.

ROW 3: (RS) Ssk, k0 (0, 0, 1, 0), k2tog (k3tog, k2tog, k3tog, k3tog), k0 (1, 1, 1, 1), sl m, k1, sssk, knit to 4 sts before next m, k3tog, k1, sl m, k0 (1, 1, 1, 1), ssk (sssk, ssk, sssk, sssk), k0 (0, 0, 1, 0), k2tog—30 (36, 38, 44, 44) sts rem; 26 (30, 32, 36, 38) back sts; 2 (3, 3, 4, 3) sts each front.

ROW 4: Purl.

ROW 5: Ssk, k0 (1, 1, 2, 1), sl m, k1, sssk, knit to 4 sts before next m, k3tog, k1, sl m, k0 (1, 1, 2, 1), k2tog—24 (30, 32, 38, 38) sts rem; 22 (26, 28, 32, 34) back sts; 1 (2, 2, 3, 2) st(s) each front.

ROW 6: Purl, removing markers.

ROW 7: Ssk, k0 (1, 1, 2, 1), sssk, k14 (18, 20, 24, 26), k3tog, k0 (1, 1, 2, 1), k2tog—18 (24, 26, 32, 32) sts rem.

ROW 8: Purl.

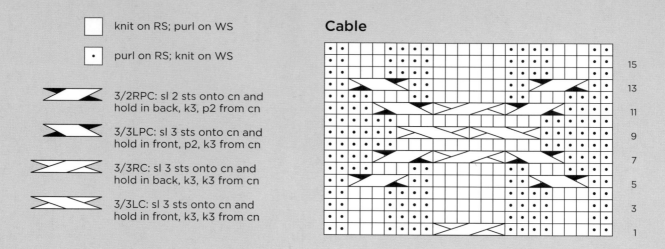

□ knit on RS; purl on WS

· purl on RS; knit on WS

3/2RPC: sl 2 sts onto cn and hold in back, k3, p2 from cn

3/3LPC: sl 3 sts onto cn and hold in front, p2, k3 from cn

3/3RC: sl 3 sts onto cn and hold in back, k3, k3 from cn

3/3LC: sl 3 sts onto cn and hold in front, k3, k3 from cn

Cable

ROW 9: Ssk, sssk, knit to last 5 sts, k3tog, k2tog—6 sts dec'd.

ROW 10: Purl.

Rep the last 2 rows 0 (1, 1, 2, 2) more time(s)—12 (12, 14, 14, 14) sts rem; yoke measures 6¼ (6¾, 7¼, 7½, 7¾)" (16 [17, 18.5, 19, 19.5] cm) from pick-up row at center back neck.

BO all sts.

FINISHING

Weave in loose ends.

Buttonhole Band

With RS facing, pick up and knit 67 (70, 73, 76, 79) sts evenly spaced along right front edge. Purl 2 rows, knit 2 rows, purl 2 rows, knit 1 row, ending with a WS row.

BUTTONHOLE ROW: (RS) K37 (38, 39, 40, 41), [k2tog, yo twice, ssk, k8 (9, 10, 11, 12)] 2 times, k2tog, yo twice, ssk, k2.

NEXT ROW: (WS) Purl, working [k1, p1] in each double yo of previous row.

Purl 1 RS row.

BO all sts kwise.

Buttonband

With RS facing, pick up and knit 67 (70, 73, 76, 79) sts evenly spaced along left front edge. [Purl 2 rows, knit 2 rows] 2 times, purl 2 rows, ending with a RS row.

BO all sts kwise.

Collar

With RS facing, pick up and knit 67 (79, 83, 89, 91) sts evenly around neck edge. Purl 1 WS row.

NEXT ROW: (RS) Work Row 1 of Cable chart over 24 sts, pm, k19 (31, 35, 41, 43), pm, work Row 1 of chart over rem 24 sts.

Cont cable patt on 24 sts at each end and working sts in center section between m in St st, work Rows 2–16 of chart, then work Rows 1–4 once more. Knit 1 WS row, then purl 1 RS row for fold line—collar measures 4¼" (11 cm) from pick-up row.

Purl 1 WS row, dec 1 (1, 1, 3, 1) st(s) in last row—66 (78, 82, 86, 90) sts rem.

NEXT ROW: (RS) K2, *p2, k2; rep from * to end.

NEXT ROW: (WS) P2, *k2, p2; rep from * to end.

Rep the last 2 rows until collar measures 4¼" (11 cm) from second row of fold line.

BO all sts in rib patt.

Fold collar to WS. With yarn threaded on a tapestry needle, sew BO row of collar to pick-up row on WS. Sew short seam at each end of collar.

Lightly steam-block, taking care not to flatten the cables. Sew buttons to left front, opposite buttonholes.

In addition to the beautiful tailoring I like to include in all of my men's designs, I wanted to add an elegant yet sporty look to this bulky jacket. The overall moss-stitch pattern with rope cable accents sings the same tune as Deille (page 30), but in a completely different voice. To add strength and stability, I added cables along the tops of the shoulders as well. This simple and masculine design is a recipe for maximum knitting and wearing enjoyment.

ERIK

FINISHED SIZE

38 (44, 47½, 54½, 60¾)" (96.5 [112, 120.5, 138.5, 154.5] cm) chest circumference, with 2 (2, 2½, 2½, 2¾)" (5 [5, 6.5, 6.5, 7] cm) front bands overlapped.

Sweater shown measures 47½" (120.5 cm).

YARN

Chunky weight (#5 Bulky).

Shown here: Cascade Ecological Wool (100% undyed Peruvian wool; 478 yd [438 m]/250 g): #8018 gray, 4 (4, 4, 5, 5) skeins.

NEEDLES

Body and sleeves: size U.S. 10 (6 mm).

Front bands, cuffs, and collar: size U.S. 7 (4.5 mm).

Adjust needle size if necessary to obtain the correct gauge.

NOTIONS

Cable needle (cn); markers (m); removable markers or waste yarn; stitch holders; tapestry needle; six ¾" (2 cm) buttons.

GAUGE

15 sts and 23 rows = 4" (10 cm) in moss stitch on larger needles.

15 sts and 36 rows = 4" (10 cm) in double garter stitch on larger needles, with garter ridges relaxed.

10 sts of right and left cable panels measure 1¾" (4.5 cm) wide on larger needles.

stitch guide

MOSS STITCH
(EVEN NUMBER OF STS)

Set-up row: (WS) *K1, p1; rep from *.

Row 1: (RS) *K1, p1; rep from *.

Rows 2 and 3: *P1, k1; rep from *.

Row 4: *K1, p1; rep from *.

Rep Rows 1–4 for pattern; do not rep the set-up row.

DOUBLE GARTER STITCH

Row 1: (RS) Purl.

Rows 2 and 3: Knit.

Row 4: Purl.

Rep Rows 1–4 for pattern.

RIGHT CABLE
(PANEL OF 10 STS)

Set-up row: (WS) K2, p6, k2.

Row 1: (RS) P2, sl 3 sts onto cable needle (cn) and hold in back, k3, k3 from cn, p2.

Row 2: K2, p6, k2.

Row 3: P2, k6, p2.

Row 4: Rep Row 2.

Rep Rows 1–4 for pattern; do not rep the Set-up row.

LEFT CABLE
(PANEL OF 10 STS)

Set-up row: (WS) K2, p6, k2.

Row 1: (RS) P2, sl 3 sts onto cable needle (cn) and hold in front, k3, k3 from cn, p2.

Row 2: K2, p6, k2.

Row 3: P2, k6, p2.

Row 4: Rep Row 2.

Rep Rows 1–4 for pattern; do not rep the Set-up row.

notes

+ The back is worked sideways in once piece, beginning at the left side and ending at the right side. Each front is worked from the side toward the center of the body. Each sleeve is worked from the cuff to the top of the sleeve cap, then sewn into the armhole during finishing.

+ The direction of the cable crossings reverses at the center of the back.

The starting row for the left cable pattern is determined by the last row worked for the right cable pattern so that their crossing rows will be equidistant from the center of the piece. If the right cable ends with Row 2, begin the left cable with Row 3—3 rows between cable crossings: Row 2 of the right cable and Rows 3 and 4 of the new left cable. If the right cable ends with

Row 4, begin the left cable with Row 3, then work Rows 2, 3, and 4 of the new left cable—7 rows between cable crossings: Rows 2, 3, and 4 of the right cable and Rows 3, 2, 3, and 4 of the new left cable.

+ The armholes are intentionally small to allow for stretch of the sideways-knitted fabric.

BACK

Left Side

With larger needles and using the long-tail method (see Glossary), CO 66 (68, 70, 72, 74) sts.

SET-UP ROW: (WS) Purl to last 10 sts, place marker (pm), work set-up row of right cable (see Stitch Guide) over last 10 sts.

NEXT ROW: (RS) Work Row 1 of right cable over 10 sts, slip marker (sl m), work Row 1 of double garter st (see Stitch Guide) to end.

Cont in patt as established, work Rows 2–4 of patts once, then rep Rows 1–4 of patts 1 (2, 2, 3, 4) more time(s), ending with WS Row 4 of patts—piece measures about 1 (1½, 1½, 2, 2½)" (2.5 [3.8, 3.8, 5, 6.5] cm) from CO.

Use removable markers or waste yarn to mark each end of last row completed to indicate end of left side.

Left Armhole

ROW 1: (RS) Work in established patt to last 2 sts, p1f&b (see Glossary), p1— 1 st inc'd.

ROWS 2 AND 4: (WS) Cont in patt, working new st in double garter st.

ROW 3: Work in patt to last 2 sts, k1f&b (see Glossary), k1—1 st inc'd.

Rep these 4 rows 1 (1, 1, 2, 2) more time(s), ending with WS Row 4 of patts—70 (72, 74, 78, 80) sts.

NEXT ROW: (RS) Work Row 1 of cable patt over 10 sts, sl m, knit to end, then use the cable method (see Glossary)

to CO 32 (32, 32, 34, 36) sts at end of row—102 (104, 106, 112, 116) sts; armhole shaping measures 1 (1, 1, 1½, 1½)" (2.5 [2.5, 2.5, 3.8, 3.8] cm) from marked row at end of side.

Left Shoulder

SET-UP ROW: (WS) Work set-up row of right cable over 10 sts, pm, work set-up row of moss st (see Stitch Guide) over 14 (16, 16, 18, 20) sts, pm, work set-up row of right cable over 10 sts, pm, work set-up row of moss st over 58 (58, 60, 64, 66) sts, sl m, work Row 2 of right cable as established over last 10 sts.

NOTE: The new cables introduced at the shoulder and base of the yoke will not be on the same pattern row as the cable already in progress at the lower edge; keep track of the cables individually as necessary.

INC ROW: (RS) Work in patt to m before last 10 cable sts, k1f&b (see Glossary), sl m, work cable patt to end—1 st inc'd.

Working marked 10-st sections in cable patt and rem sts in moss st, work 3 rows even in patt, working new sts into moss st.

Rep the shaping of the last 4 rows 5 (6, 7, 8, 9) more times, then work RS inc row once more—109 (112, 115, 122, 127) sts; left shoulder measures 4½ (5¼, 6, 6½, 7¼)" (11.5 [13.5, 15, 16.5, 18.5] cm) from sts CO at end of left armhole.

Shape Back Neck

NEXT ROW: (WS) BO 10 sts, remove m, work to end of row—99 (102, 105, 112, 117) sts rem.

Cont in established patt, work 16 (16, 16, 18, 18) rows even, ending with a WS row—back neck measures 3 (3, 3, 3¼, 3¼)" (7.5 [7.5, 7.5, 8.5, 8.5] cm) from sts BO for neck shaping; piece measures 9½ (10¾, 11½, 13¼, 14½)" (24 [27.5, 29, 33.5, 37] cm) from CO.

NOTE: Starting on the next RS row, change to working both cable sections according to the left cable patt (see Stitch Guide), beg with the appropriate row (see Notes).

Work 16 (16, 16, 18, 18) rows even, ending with a WS row.

NEXT ROW: (RS) Work in patt to end, then use the cable method to CO 10 sts—109 (112, 115, 122, 127) sts; back neck measures 6 (6, 6, 6½, 6½)" (15 [15, 15, 16.5, 16.5] cm) from start of neck shaping.

Right Shoulder

SET-UP ROW: (WS) Work left cable over 10 new sts according to same patt row as cable at base of yoke, pm, work in established patt to end.

DEC ROW: (RS) Work in patt to 2 sts before last 10 cable sts, work either k2tog or p2tog as necessary to maintain patt, sl m, work cable patt to end— 1 st dec'd.

Work 3 rows even in patt. Rep the shaping of the last 4 rows 5 (6, 7, 8, 9) more times, then work RS dec row once more—102 (104, 106, 112, 116) sts; right shoulder measures 4½ (5¼, 6, 6½, 7¼)" (11.5 [13.5, 15, 16.5, 18.5] cm) from sts CO at end of neck shaping.

Right Armhole

NEXT ROW: (WS) BO 32 (32, 32, 34, 36) sts at beg of row while removing m as you come to them, purl to last 10 sts, sl m, work last 10 sts in established cable patt—70 (72, 74, 78, 80) sts rem.

Cont cable patts as established, change to working sts outside marked cable section in double garter st, beg with Row 1 of double garter st on foll RS row.

ROW 1: (RS) Work in patt to last 2 sts, p2tog—1 st dec'd.

ROWS 2 AND 4: (WS) Work even in patt.

ROW 3: Work in patt to last 2 sts, k2tog—1 st inc'd.

Rep these 4 rows 1 (1, 1, 2, 2) more time(s), ending with WS Row 4 of double garter st—66 (68, 70, 72, 74) sts rem; piece measures 1 (1, 1, 1½, 1½)" (2.5 [2.5, 2.5, 3.8, 3.8] cm) from sts BO for armhole.

Right Side

Mark each end of last row completed to indicate start of right side.

Cont cable patt as established, rep Rows 1–4 of double garter st 2 (3, 3, 4, 5) times.

NEXT ROW: (RS) Work 10 sts in cable patt, knit to end—piece measures about 1 (1½, 1½, 2, 2½)" (2.5 [3.8, 3.8, 5, 6.5] cm) from marked row at beg of right side and 19 (21½, 23, 26½, 29)" (48.5 [54.5, 58.5, 67.5, 73.5] cm) from starting CO.

Loosely BO all sts as they appear (knit the knits and purl the purls).

RIGHT FRONT
Right Side and Right Armhole

Work as for back left side and left armhole, ending with RS Row 1 of cable patt—102 (104, 106, 112, 116) sts; armhole shaping measures 1 (1, 1½, 1½)" (2.5 [2.5, 2.5, 3.8, 3.8] cm) from marked row at end of side and piece measures 2 (2½, 2½, 3½, 4)" (5 [6.5, 6.5, 9, 10] cm) from initial CO.

Right Shoulder and Pocket Opening

SET-UP ROW: (WS) Work set-up row of right cable over 10 sts, pm, work set-up row of moss st over 14 (16, 16, 18, 20) sts, pm, work set-up row of right cable over 10 sts, pm, work set-up row of moss st over 58 (58, 60, 64, 66) sts, sl m, work Row 2 of right cable as established over last 10 sts.

NOTE: As for the back, the new cables introduced at the shoulder and base of the yoke will not be on the same pattern row as the cable already in progress at the lower edge.

INC ROW: (RS) Work in patt to m before last 10 cable sts, k1f&b, sl m, work cable patt to end—1 st inc'd at shoulder; 103 (105, 107, 113, 117) sts.

Working marked 10-st sections in cable patt and rem sts in moss st, work 3 rows even in patt, working new sts into moss st.

Lower Body

NOTE: In order to create the diagonal pocket opening, the sts are divided above and below the pocket and worked separately, each section with its own ball of yarn. On the lower part of the body, continue established patts while increasing at the pocket edge (end of RS rows). On the upper part of the body, shoulder shaping continues at the same time as decreases at the pocket edge (beg of RS rows).

NEXT ROW: (RS; pocket dividing row) Work 10 cable sts, sl m, work 10 (11, 12, 13, 14) sts in moss st, place rem 83 (84, 85, 90, 93) sts on holder to work later for upper body—20 (21, 22, 23, 24) lower body sts rem.

Work back and forth on lower body sts only as foll:

ROW 1: (WS) Work even in patt.

ROW 2: (RS) Work in patt to last st, k1f&b—1 st inc'd at pocket edge.

Rep the shaping of the last 2 rows 7 (7, 9, 9, 9) more times, ending with a RS row—28 (29, 32, 33, 34) sts; piece measures 3 (3, 3¾, 3¾, 3¾)" (7.5 [7.5, 9.5, 9.5 9.5] cm) from pocket dividing row, measured straight up along a single column of sts (do not measure along diagonal pocket edge).

Cut yarn, leaving a 10" (25.5 cm) tail. Place these sts on holder to work later.

Upper Body

Return 83 (84, 85, 90, 93) held upper body sts to needle and rejoin yarn with RS facing, ready to work a RS row.

NEXT ROW: (RS; shoulder inc row) Work in patt to m before last 10 cable sts, k1f&b, sl m, work cable patt to end—1 st inc'd at shoulder.

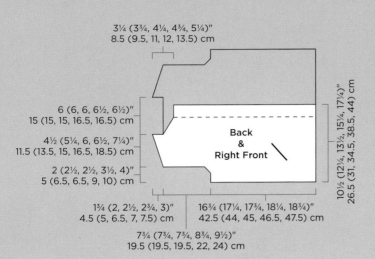

3¼ (3¾, 4¼, 4¾, 5¼)"
8.5 (9.5, 11, 12, 13.5) cm

6 (6, 6, 6½, 6½)"
15 (15, 15, 16.5, 16.5) cm

4½ (5¼, 6, 6½, 7¼)"
11.5 (13.5, 15, 16.5, 18.5) cm

2 (2½, 2½, 3½, 4)"
5 (6.5, 6.5, 9, 10) cm

Back & Right Front

10½ (12¼, 13½, 15¼, 17¼)"
26.5 (31, 34.5, 38.5, 44) cm

1¾ (2, 2½, 2¾, 3)"
4.5 (5, 6.5, 7, 7.5) cm

16¾ (17¼, 17¾, 18¼, 18¾)"
42.5 (44, 45, 46.5, 47.5) cm

7¾ (7¾, 7¾, 8¾, 9½)"
19.5 (19.5, 19.5, 22, 24) cm

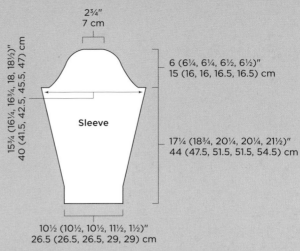

2¾"
7 cm

15¾ (16¼, 16¾, 18, 18½)"
40 (41.5, 42.5, 45.5, 47) cm

Sleeve

6 (6¼, 6¼, 6½, 6½)"
15 (16, 16, 16.5, 16.5) cm

17¼ (18¾, 20¼, 20¼, 21½)"
44 (47.5, 51.5, 51.5, 54.5) cm

10½ (10½, 10½, 11½, 1½)"
26.5 (26.5, 26.5, 29, 29) cm

ROW 1: (WS) Work even in patt, working new st at shoulder into moss st.

ROW 2: (RS; pocket dec row) K2tog, work in patt to end—1 st dec'd at pocket edge.

ROW 3: Work even in patt.

ROW 4: K2tog, work in patt to m before last 10 cable sts, k1f&b, sl m, work in patt to end—1 st dec'd for pocket, 1 st inc'd for shoulder, no change to st count.

Rep the last 4 rows 3 (3, 4, 4, 4) more times—80 (81, 81, 86, 89) sts; 5 (5, 6, 6, 6) sts total inc'd at shoulder; 8 (8, 10, 10, 10) sts total dec'd at pocket edge; piece measures 3 (3, 3¾, 3¾, 3¾)" (7.5 [7.5, 9.5, 9.5 9.5] cm) from pocket dividing row.

Do not cut yarn.

Join Upper and Lower Body

With WS facing and using yarn attached to upper body, work in patt across 80 (81, 81, 86, 89) upper body sts, return 28 (29, 32, 33, 34) lower body sts to needle, work across lower body sts to end—108 (110, 113, 119, 123) sts total.

Work 2 rows even in patt, ending with a WS row. [Work the RS shoulder inc row from before pocket opening once, then work 3 rows even in patt] 0 (1, 1, 2, 3) time(s), then work shoulder inc row once more, ending with a RS inc row and working new sts into moss st—109 (112, 115, 122, 127) sts; right shoulder measures 4½ (5¼, 6, 6½, 7¼)" (11.5 [13.5, 15, 16.5, 18.5 cm) from sts CO at end of right armhole.

Shape Front Neck

NEXT ROW: (WS) BO 10 (11, 12, 13, 14) sts, work in patt to end—99 (101, 103, 109, 113) sts rem.

ROW 1: (RS) Work in patt to last 3 sts, k2tog, k1—1 st dec'd at neck edge.

ROW 2: Work even in patt.

Rep the last 2 rows 4 (5, 5, 6, 7) more times, then work RS Row 1 once more—93 (94, 96, 101, 104) sts rem; front neck measures 2 (2½, 2½, 2¾, 3¼)" (5 [6.5, 6.5, 7, 8.5] cm) from sts BO at start of neck shaping; piece measures 8½ (10¼, 11, 12¾, 14½)" (21.5 [26, 28, 32.5, 37] cm) from starting CO.

Buttonband

Change to smaller needles and purl 1 WS row.

Work Rows 1–4 of double garter st 4 (4, 5, 5, 6) times, ending with WS Row 4. Purl 1 RS row—buttonband measures about 2 (2, 2½, 2½, 2¾)" (5 [5, 6.5, 6.5, 7] cm); piece measures about 10½ (12¼, 13½, 15¼, 17¼)" (26.5 [31, 34.5, 38.5, 44] cm) from starting CO.

With WS facing, BO all sts kwise.

LEFT FRONT

Left Side

With larger needles and using the long-tail method, CO 66 (68, 70, 72, 74) sts.

SET-UP ROW: (WS) Work set-up row for left cable over first 10 sts, pm, purl to end.

NEXT ROW: (RS) Work Row 1 of double garter st to m, sl m, work Row 1 of left cable over 10 sts.

Cont in patt as established, work Rows 2–4 of patts once, then rep Rows 1–4 of patts 1 (2, 2, 3, 4) more time(s), ending with WS Row 4 of patts—piece measures about 1 (1½, 1½, 2, 2½)" (2.5 [3.8, 3.8, 5, 6.5] cm) from CO.

Using removable markers or waste yarn, mark each end of last row completed to indicate end of left side.

Left Armhole

ROW 1: (RS) P1, p1f&b, work in established patt to end—1 st inc'd.

ROWS 2 AND 4: (WS) Cont in patt, working new st in double garter st.

ROW 3: K1, k1f&b, work in patt to end—1 st inc'd.

Rep these 4 rows 1 (1, 1, 2, 2) more time(s), ending with WS Row 4 of patts—70 (72, 74, 78, 80) sts.

NEXT ROW: (RS) Use the cable method to CO 32 (32, 32, 34, 36) sts, knit across new sts, knit to m, sl m, work Row 1 of cable patt over 10 sts—102 (104, 106, 112, 116) sts; armhole shaping measures 1 (1, 1, 1½, 1½)" (2.5 [2.5, 2.5 3,8, 3.8] cm) from marked row at end of side.

Left Shoulder and Pocket Opening

SET-UP ROW: (WS) Work Row 2 of left cable as established over 10 sts, sl m, work set-up row of moss st over 58 (58, 60, 64, 66) sts, pm, work set-up row of left cable over 10 sts, pm, work set-up row of moss st over 14 (16, 16, 18, 20) sts, pm, work set-up row of left cable over last 10 sts.

NOTE: As for the back and right front, the new cables introduced at the shoulder and base of the yoke will not be on the same pattern row as the cable at the lower edge.

INC ROW: (RS) Work 10 sts in cable patt, sl m, k1f&b, work in patt to end—1 st inc'd at shoulder—103 (105, 107, 113, 117) sts.

Working marked 10-st sections in cable patt and rem sts in moss st, work 3 rows even in patt, working new sts into moss st.

Upper Body

NOTE: As for the right front, the sts are divided above and below the diagonal pocket opening and worked separately, each section with its own ball of yarn. On the lower part of the body, continue established patts while increasing at the pocket edge (beg of RS rows). On the upper part of the body, shoulder shaping continues at the same time as decreases at the pocket edge (end of RS rows).

NEXT ROW: (RS; pocket dividing row) Work 10 sts in cable patt, sl m, k1f&b, work 72 (73, 74, 79, 82) more moss sts, place rem 20 (21, 22, 23, 24) sts on holder to work later for lower body—1 st inc'd at shoulder—84 (85, 86, 91, 94) upper body sts.

ROW 1: (WS) Work even in patt, working new st at shoulder into moss st.

ROW 2: (RS; pocket dec row) Work in patt to last 2 sts, ssk—1 st dec'd at pocket edge.

ROW 3: Work even in patt.

ROW 4: Work 10 sts in cable patt, sl m, k1f&b, work in patt to last 2 sts, ssk—1 st dec'd for pocket, 1 st inc'd for shoulder, no change to st count.

Rep the last 4 rows 3 (3, 4, 4, 4) more times—80 (81, 81, 86, 89) sts; 5 (5, 6, 6, 6) sts total inc'd at shoulder; 8 (8, 10, 10, 10) sts total dec'd at pocket edge; piece measures 3 (3, 3¾, 3¾, 3¾)" (7.5 [7.5, 9.5, 9.5 9.5] cm) from pocket dividing row.

Cut yarn, leaving a 10" (25.5 cm) tail, and place these sts on holder to work later.

Lower Body

Return 20 (21, 22, 23, 24) held lower body sts to needle and rejoin yarn with RS facing, ready to work a RS row.

NEXT ROW: (RS) Work in patt to end.

ROW 1: (WS) Work even in patt.

ROW 2: (RS) K1f&b, work in patt to end—1 st inc'd at pocket edge.

Rep the shaping of the last 2 rows 7 (7, 9, 9, 9) more times, ending with a RS row—28 (29, 32, 33, 34) sts; piece measures 3 (3, 3¾, 3¾, 3¾)" (7.5 [7.5,

9.5, 9.5, 9.5] cm) from pocket dividing row, measured straight up along a single column of sts (do not measure along diagonal pocket edge).

Do not cut yarn.

Join Upper and Lower Body

NEXT ROW: (WS) With WS facing and using yarn attached to lower body, work in patt across 28 (29, 32, 33, 34) lower body sts, return 80 (81, 81, 86, 89) sts of the held upper body sts to needle, work across upper body sts to end—108 (110, 113, 119, 123) sts total.

Work 2 rows even in patt, ending with a WS row.

[Work the RS shoulder inc row from before pocket opening once, then work 3 rows even in patt] 0 (1, 1, 2, 3) time(s), then work shoulder inc row once more, ending with a RS inc row and working new sts into moss st—109 (112, 115, 122, 127) sts; left shoulder measures 4½ (5¼, 6, 6½, 7¼)" (11.5 [13.5, 15, 16.5, 18.5 cm) from sts CO at end of left armhole.

Shape Front Neck

NEXT ROW: (WS) Work even in patt.

NEXT ROW: (RS) BO 10 (11, 12, 13, 14) sts, work in patt to end—99 (101, 103, 109, 113) sts rem.

ROW 1: (WS) Work even in patt.

ROW 2: (RS) K1, ssk, work in patt to end—1 st dec'd at neck edge.

Rep the last 2 rows 5 (6, 6, 7, 8) more times—93 (94, 96, 101, 104) sts rem; front neck measures 2 (2½, 2½, 2¾, 3¼)" (5 [6.5, 6.5, 7, 8.5] cm) from sts BO at

start of neck shaping; piece measures 8½ (10¼, 11, 12¾, 14½)" (21.5 [26, 28, 32.5, 37] cm) from starting CO.

Buttonhole Band

Change to smaller needles and purl 1 WS row. Work Rows 1–4 of double garter st 2 (2, 2, 2, 3) times, ending with WS Row 4.

BUTTONHOLE ROW: (RS; Row 1 of patt) P7 (7, 9, 9, 10) *p2tog, yo, p14 (14, 14, 15, 15); rep from * 4 more times, p2tog, yo, p4 (5, 5, 5, 7)— 6 buttonholes.

Work Rows 2–4 of patt, then rep Rows 1–4 of patt 1 (1, 2, 2, 2) more times(s), ending with WS Row 4.

Purl 1 RS row—buttonband measures about 2 (2, 2½, 2½, 2¾)" (5 [5, 6.5, 6.5, 7] cm); piece measures about 10½ (12¼, 13½, 15¼, 17¼)" (26.5 [31, 34.5, 38.5, 44] cm) from starting CO.

BO all sts kwise with WS facing.

SLEEVES

With smaller needles, CO 42 (42, 42, 46, 46) sts. Purl 1 WS row. Rep Rows 1–4 of double garter st 6 times, ending with WS Row 4 of patt—piece measures about 2¾" (7 cm) from CO.

NEXT ROW: (RS) Knit, inc 4 sts evenly spaced—46 (46, 46, 50, 50) sts.

SET-UP ROW: (WS) Work set-up row of moss st over 6 (6, 6, 8, 8) sts, pm, work set-up row of left cable over 10 sts, pm, work set-up row of moss st over center 14 sts, pm, work set-up row of right cable over 10 sts, pm, work set-up row of moss st over 6 (6, 6, 8, 8) sts.

Change to larger needles and shape sleeve as foll:

ROWS 1–4: Work 4 rows even as established, ending with a WS row.

ROW 5: (RS; inc row) Work in patt to end of first cable section, sl m, work [k1, p1] in next st, work in moss st to 1 st before next m, work [k1, p1] in next st, sl m, work in patt to end—2 sts inc'd in center section.

ROWS 6–8: Work 3 rows even in patt, working new sts into moss st patt and ending with a WS row.

Rep these 8 rows 9 (10, 11, 11, 12) more times, then work Rows 1–4 once more, ending with a WS row—66 (68, 70, 74, 76) sts; 34 (36, 38, 38, 40) moss sts in center section; piece measures about 17¼ (18¾, 20¼, 20¼, 21½)" (44 [47.5, 51.5, 51.5, 54.5] cm) from CO. For a longer sleeve, cont even in patt until desired length, ending with a WS row.

Shape Cap

BO 8 (9, 10, 11, 12) sts at beg of next 2 rows—50 (50, 50, 52, 52) sts rem.

DEC ROW: (RS) K2, ssk, work in moss to last 4 sts, k2tog, k2—2 sts dec'd.

NEXT ROW: (WS) P3, work in patt to last 3 sts, p3.

Rep the last 2 rows 4 (6, 6, 7, 7) more times—40 (36, 36, 36, 36) sts. [Rep dec row, work 3 rows even] 2 times, work dec row once more, then work 1 WS row—34 (30, 30, 30, 30) sts rem.

DOUBLE DEC ROW: (RS) K2, sl 1 kwise with yarn in back, k2tog, psso, work in patt to last 5 sts, k3tog, k2—4 sts dec'd.

Cont in patt, rep the double dec row every RS row 5 (4, 4, 4, 4) times, then work 1 WS row even after last double dec row—10 sts rem for all sizes.

BO all sts in patt, working the first and last 5 sts of the BO row as for the double dec row.

FINISHING

Weave in loose ends. Steam-block pieces to measurements.

With yarn threaded on a tapestry needle, sew fronts to back at shoulders. Sew sleeve caps into armholes, then sew sleeve and side seams.

Collar

With smaller needles, RS facing, and beg at right front BO edge, pick up and knit 30 (32, 32, 33, 34) sts evenly spaced to shoulder seam, 32 (32, 32, 34, 36) sts across back neck, and 30 (32, 32, 33, 34) sts to left front BO edge—92 (96, 96, 100, 104) sts total. Knit 2 rows, purl 1 row, ending with a WS row.

Work Rows 1–4 of double garter st 6 times, then work Rows 1 and 2 once more, ending with a WS row—collar measures about 3¼" (8.5 cm) from pick-up row.

NEXT ROW: (RS) K1, *p2, k2; rep from * to last 3 sts, p2, k1.

Work sts as they appear until rib section of collar measures 3¼" (8.5 cm).

BO all sts in rib patt.

Fold ribbed facing to inside and, with yarn threaded on a tapestry needle, sew BO edge to pick-up ridge on WS of neck. Sew short seams at ends of collar.

Pockets

Welts (make 2)

With smaller needles and RS facing, pick up and knit 23 (23, 28, 28, 28) sts evenly spaced along lower edge of pocket opening. Work 8 rows in Rev St st (purl RS rows, knit WS rows), ending with a RS row.

Loosely BO off all sts.

Cut yarn, leaving a 12" (30.5 cm) tail. Fold the 8 rows in half so the purl side faces outward. With yarn threaded on a tapestry needle, sew BO edge to pick-up ridge on WS of garment, then sew short seams at ends of welt.

Pocket Linings (make 2)

With smaller needles and RS facing, pick up and knit 23 (23, 28, 28, 28) sts evenly spaced along upper edge of pocket opening. Work even in St st for 9" (23 cm).

Loosely BO all sts.

Fold lining in half with RS facing tog (WS facing out) and sew lining side seams. Sew BO edge of lining to base of welt on WS of garment. Tack ends of welts to RS of fronts.

Block again if desired to set seams. Sew buttons to right front, opposite buttonholes.

three
EVERY WHICH WAY

Internal increases and decreases, short-rows that pivot on a point, knitting on the bias, complex combinations of traveling cables in collusion with both short-rows and full fashioning—this chapter has it all! For these four designs, I simply decided to throw all the techniques "in the pot" and see what materialized. These garments include a mixture of knitting directions and more involved combinations of the techniques that have been used in other chapters. Each piece is a little masterwork in its own right.

Merideth (page 112) is worked in two pieces that begin at the wrist and end at the center of the body. Then the skirt is knitted separately (also sideways). The back of the bodice is eased along the skirt to create a slouchy, relaxed look. The fronts of **Felix** (page 120) also begin at the side seams, but they take a detour at the center front where the decorative cable pattern at the hem

turns the corner and continues along the vertical front edge. The "normal-looking" sleeves are actually knitted from the top down.

Beginning at the shoulder, **Jacqui** (page 130) is shaped with a combination of short-rows and increases that causes the knitting to be truly sideways at the side seams. The back is knitted separately, then the pieces are seamed

at the shoulders and sides. If you prefer to omit a seam, you could continue one front across the back to the opposite side seam.

I consider **Jose** (page 140) the high point of this collection, because it requires some degree of knitting expertise. This shaping involves a crucial set of short-rows in the middle of the complex traveling cable design.

Relaxed and casual, this swing coat has a bohemian look. The bodice is composed of two pieces, each worked from the wrist to the center of the body. The pieces are seamed together at the center back, then the skirt is knitted separately (from side to side, of course!) and shaped with three short-row sections to add flare to the hem. Finally, the skirt is sewn to the bodice, with fullness gathered in across the back.

MERIDETH

FINISHED SIZE

40½ (50½, 57½)" (103 [128.5, 146] cm) bust circumference. Garment is styled for an oversized fit; see Notes.

Sweater shown measures 40½" (103 cm).

YARN

Worsted weight (#4 Medium).

Shown here: Tahki/Stacy Charles Tivoli (52% silk, 48% kid mohair; 108 yd [99 m]/50 g): #02 taupe, 11 (14, 16) balls.

NEEDLES

Body and sleeves: size U.S. 9 (5.5 mm): 24" (60 cm) circular (cir).

Neckband: size U.S. 7 (4.5 mm).

Adjust needle size if necessary to obtain the correct gauge.

NOTIONS

Markers (m); removable markers or waste yarn; stitch holder; tapestry needle.

GAUGE

16 sts and 24 rows = 4" (10 cm) in St st on larger needles.

15 sts and 28 rows = 4" (10 cm) in garter rib pattern on larger needles.

16 sts and 28 rows = 4" (10 cm) in moss stitch on larger needles.

28 (30, 32) sts in bias St st of lower sleeves measure about 5 (5¼, 5¾)" (12.5 [13.5, 14.5] cm) wide on larger needles (see Notes).

stitch guide

DOUBLE GARTER STITCH

Row 1: (RS) Purl.

Rows 2 (WS) and 3 (RS): Knit.

Row 4: Purl.

Rep Rows 1–4 for pattern.

GARTER RIB PATTERN (MULTIPLE OF 4 STS + 2)

Row 1: (RS) K2, *p2, k2; rep from *.

Row 2: (WS) Purl.

Rep Rows 1 and 2 for pattern.

MOSS STITCH (ODD NUMBER OF STS)

Row 1: (RS) P1, *k1, p1; rep from *.

Row 2 (WS) and Row 3 (RS): K1, *p1, k1; rep from *.

Row 4: Rep Row 1.

Rep Rows 1–4 for pattern.

notes

+ This is a loose-fitting, draped garment; it should be worn with about 4" to 6" (10 to 15 cm) positive ease.

+ The sleeves and upper body are worked sideways in two mirror-image halves, each beginning at the cuff and ending in the center of the body. The skirt is worked separately from side to side with short-rows to add flare to the lower edge, then sewn to the assembled upper body during finishing.

+ To check the bias stockinette gauge for the lower sleeves, do not measure along the diagonal columns of stitches. Instead, lay a ruler across the bias section at a 90-degree angle to the center stitch and selvedges, and measure the width of the 28 (30, 32) stitches between the center stitch and the selvedge at the end of RS rows, not including the center stitch.

+ The second stitch of a k1f&b increase creates a "pip" on the right side of the fabric. Working the k1f&b increases in the stitches on each side of the marked center stitch creates the appearance of 2 knit stitches between the "pips": the center stitch itself, and the k1 part of the k1f&b increase that follows it. At the shoulder, these 2 knit stitches will become the center k2 column of the garter rib pattern.

+ The schematic for this project does not show the garment parts oriented in the direction of the knitting.

LEFT HALF

Sleeve

With smaller needles, CO 56 (60, 64) sts. Knit 5 rows, beg and ending with a WS row—3 garter ridges on RS.

NEXT ROW: Change to larger cir needle and with RS facing, k1, ssk, k23 (25, 27), k1f&b (see Glossary), place marker (pm), k1, pm, k1f&b, k23 (25, 27), k2tog, k2— no change to st count; 27 (29, 31) sts before marked st; 28 (30, 32) sts after marked st; decs at each end of row are deliberately not the same distance from the selvedges.

NEXT ROW: (WS) Purl.

Rep the last 2 rows until piece measures 13 (13½, 14)" (33 [34.5, 35.5] cm) from CO, measured straight up along the marked center st, ending with a WS row.

Mark each end of last row completed to indicate end of sleeve.

Upper Body

Change to double garter st (see Stitch Guide) and cont incs on each side of center st without any further decs as foll:

INC ROW: (RS) Work in double garter st to 1 st before m, work k1f&b or p1f&b (see Glossary) as necessary to maintain patt, slip marker (sl m), work center st in double garter patt, sl m, work k1f&b or p1f&b as necessary to maintain patt,

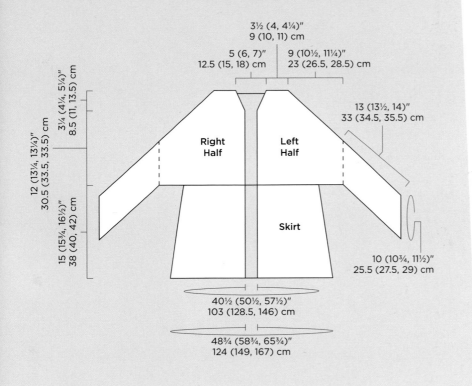

3½ (4, 4¼)"
9 (10, 11) cm

5 (6, 7)" **9 (10½, 11¼)"**
12.5 (15, 18) cm **23 (26.5, 28.5) cm**

3¼ (4¼, 5¼)"
8.5 (11, 13.5) cm

12 (13¼, 13¼)"
30.5 (33.5, 33.5) cm

Right Half

Left Half

13 (13½, 14)"
33 (34.5, 35.5) cm

15 (15¾, 16½)"
38 (40, 42) cm

Skirt

10 (10¾, 11½)"
25.5 (27.5, 29) cm

40½ (50½, 57½)"
103 (128.5, 146) cm

48¾ (58¾, 65¾)"
124 (149, 167) cm

work in double garter st to end—2 sts inc'd; 1 st on each side of center.

NEXT ROW: (WS) Work even in double garter st.

Rep the last 2 rows 4 more times, ending with Row 2 of double garter patt—66 (70, 74) sts; 32 (34, 36) sts before marked st; 33 (35, 37) sts after marked st; piece measures 1¾" (4.5 cm) from marked row at end of sleeve, measured along selvedges.

Change to moss st (see Stitch Guide) and garter rib patt (as defined below) and cont to inc on each side of center st as foll:

ROW 1: (RS) K2, work moss st over 7 sts, *k2, p2; rep from * to 3 (1, 3) sts before m, k2 (0, 2), k1f&b, sl m, k1, sl m, k1f&b, p1 (0, 1), k2 (1, 2), **p2, k2; rep from ** to last 9 sts, work moss st over 7 sts, k2—2 sts inc'd.

ROWS 2, 4, AND 6: (WS) P2, moss st over 7 sts, purl to m, sl m, p1, sl m, purl to last 9 sts, work moss st over 7 sts, p2.

ROW 3: K2, work 7 moss sts, *k2, p2; rep from * to 4 (2, 4) sts before m, k2 (1, 2), p1 (0, 1), k1f&b, sl m, k1, sl m, k1f&b, k0 (2, 0), **p2, k2; rep from ** to last 9 sts, work 7 moss sts, k2—2 sts inc'd.

ROW 5: K2, work 7 moss sts, *k2, p2; rep from * to 1 (3, 1) st(s) before m, k0 (2, 0), k1f&b, sl m, k1, sl m, k1f&b, p0 (1, 0), k1 (2, 1), **p2, k2; rep from ** to last 9 sts, work 7 moss sts, k2—2 sts inc'd.

ROW 7: K2, work 7 moss sts, *k2, p2; rep from * to 2 (4, 2) sts before m, k1 (2, 1), p0 (1, 0), k1f&b, sl m, k1, sl m, k1f&b, k2 (0, 2), **p2, k2; rep from ** to last 9 sts, work 7 moss sts, k2—2 sts inc'd.

ROW 8: Rep Row 2.

Rep the last 8 rows 5 (6, 7) more times, then work the first 2 (6, 2) rows once more, ending with WS Row 2 (6, 2)—116 (132, 140) sts; piece measures 9 (10½, 11¼)" (23 [26.5, 28.5] cm) from end of sleeve.

NEXT ROW: (RS) K2, work 7 moss sts, work Row 1 of garter rib patt over center 98 (114, 122) sts, removing m on each side of center st as you come to them, work 7 moss sts, k2.

Cont in established patts with no further incs for 3½ (4, 4¼)" (9 [10, 11] cm) more, ending with a WS row—piece measures 12½ (14½, 15½)" (31.5 [37, 39.5] cm) from end of sleeve.

Front Neck

DIVIDING ROW: (RS) Work 56 (64, 68) sts in patt for back, BO 10 (12, 14) sts, work in patt to end for front—56 (64, 68) back sts; 50 (56, 58) front sts.

If desired, place back sts on holder while working front neck shaping.

Working on front sts only, dec 1 st at neck edge (beg of RS rows) on the next 4 (6, 8) RS rows, then work 1 WS row even after the last dec row—46 (50, 50) front sts rem; neck shaping measures 1½ (2, 2½)" (3.8 [5, 6.5] cm) from dividing row; piece measures 14 (16½, 18)" (35.5 [42, 45.5] cm) from end of sleeve.

BO all sts firmly.

Back Neck

Return 56 (64, 68) back sts to needle, if they are not already on the needle, and join yarn with WS facing. Work even in patt until back neck measures 2½ (3, 3½)" (6.5 [7.5, 9] cm) from dividing row, ending with a WS row—piece measures 15 (17½, 19)" (38 [44.5, 48.5] cm) from end of sleeve.

BO all sts firmly.

RIGHT HALF

Work as for left half to start of front neck shaping—116 (132, 140) sts; piece measures 12½ (14½, 15½)" (31.5 [37, 39.5] cm) from end of sleeve.

Back Neck

DIVIDING ROW: (RS) Work 50 (56, 58) sts in patt for front, BO 10 (12, 14) sts, work in patt to end for back—50 (56, 58) front sts; 56 (64, 68) back sts.

If desired, place front sts on holder while working back neck. Working on back sts only, work even in patt until back neck measures 2½ (3, 3½)" (6.5 [7.5, 9] cm) from dividing row, ending with a WS row—piece measures 15 (17½, 19)" (38 [44.5, 48.5] cm) from end of sleeve.

BO all sts firmly.

Front Neck

Return 50 (56, 58) front sts to needle, if they are not already on the needle, and join yarn with WS facing. Working on front sts only, dec 1 st at neck edge (end of RS rows) on the next 4 (6, 8) RS rows, then work 1 WS row even after the last dec row—46 (50, 50) front sts rem; neck shaping measures 1½ (2, 2½)" (3.8 [5, 6.5] cm) from dividing row; piece measures 14 (16½, 18)" (35.5 [42, 45.5] cm) from end of sleeve.

BO all sts firmly.

SKIRT

With larger cir needle, CO 60 (63, 66) sts. Purl 1 WS row.

Cont as foll:

ROW 1: (RS) K2, work 7 sts in moss st, knit to end.

ROW 2: (WS) Purl to last 9 sts, work 7 sts in moss st, p2.

Rep Rows 1 and 2 until piece measures 9 (11½, 13¼)" (23 [29, 33.5] cm) from CO, ending with a WS row.

Mark each end of last row completed.

Short-row Panel

Work short-rows (see Glossary) to flare lower edge as foll:

ROW 1: (RS) K2, work 7 moss sts, wrap next st, turn work.

ROWS 2, 4, 6, 8, AND 10: (WS) Work in established patts to end.

ROWS 3, 5, 7, 9, AND 11: K2, work 7 moss sts, knit to previously wrapped st, work wrap tog with wrapped st, k7,

wrap next st, turn—wrapped st in Row 11 is the 41st St st and 50th st from beg of row.

ROW 12: Rep Row 2.

ROWS 13–20: Working rem wrap tog with wrapped st as you come to it, work 8 rows even in patt.

ROWS 21–32: Rep Rows 1–12 once more—short-row panel measures 4½" (11.5 cm) from marked row at lower edge (beg of RS rows) and 1¼" (3.2 cm) from marked row at upper edge (end of RS rows).

Mark each end of last row completed to indicate end of first short-row panel.

Working rem wrap tog with wrapped st as you come to it, work even in patt until piece measures 10 (12½, 14¼)" (25.5 [31.5, 36] cm) from end of first short-row panel. Work Rows 1–12 only of short-row panel—piece measures 25¼ (30¼, 33¾)" (64 [77, 85.5] cm) from CO at lower edge and 20¼ (25¼, 28¾)" (51.5 [64, 73] cm) from CO at upper edge.

Mark the upper edge of the last row completed to indicate middle of skirt.

Working rem wrap tog with wrapped st as you come to it, work even in patt until piece measures 10 (12½, 14¼)" (25.5 [31.5, 36] cm) from end of 12-row short-row panel in middle of skirt. Work Rows 1–32 of full short-row panel, then work 9 (11½, 13¼)" (23 [29, 33.5] cm) from end of second full short-row panel, ending with a WS row—skirt measures 48¾ (58¾, 65¾)" (124 [149, 167] cm) from CO at lower edge and 40½ (50½, 57½)" (103 [128.5, 146] cm) from CO at upper edge.

BO all sts.

FINISHING

Weave in loose ends.

Seams

With yarn threaded on a tapestry needle, sew right and left halves together at center back.

On the back and front, measure in 4" (10 cm) toward the center from marked row at end of sleeve along lower edges of the body and place removable markers—22 (27, 30)" (56 [68.5, 76] cm) between new back m; 10 (12½, 14)" (25.5 [31.5, 35.5] cm) between each new front m and front BO edge.

Beg at CO edge of sleeve, sew sleeve seam, then sew underarm seam to new m. Sew upper edge of skirt to rem lower edge of the body, aligning the marked row in middle of skirt with center back seam and easing in fullness as necessary.

Gently steam-block, taking care not to flatten the texture.

Left Front Edging

With smaller needles, RS facing, and beg at base of neck shaping, pick up and knit 102 (110, 112) sts evenly spaced along left front edge.

ROW 1: (WS) [P1, k1] 3 times, purl to end.

ROW 2: (RS) Purl to last 6 sts, work 6 rib sts as they appear (knit the knits and purl the purls).

ROW 3: Work 6 rib sts, knit to end.

ROW 4: Knit to last 6 sts, work 6 rib sts.

Work short-rows to flare lower edge as foll:

NEXT ROW: (WS) Work 6 rib sts, p7, wrap next st, turn,

NEXT ROW: (RS) Knit to last 6 sts, work 6 rib sts.

NEXT ROW: (WS) Work 6 rib sts, purl to previously wrapped st, work wrap tog with wrapped st, p7, wrap next st, turn

Rep the last 2 rows 9 (10, 11) more times—wrapped st in last WS row is the 88 (96, 104)th St st and 94 (102, 100)th st from beg of row.

NEXT ROW: (RS) Knit to last 6 sts, work 6 rib sts.

NEXT ROW: (WS) Work 6 rib sts, purl to end.

NEXT ROW: (RS) Purl to last 6 sts, work 6 rib sts—edging measures 4¾ (5, 5¼)" (12 [12.5, 13.5] cm) from pick-up row at lower edge (the edge with ribbing) and 1" (2.5 cm) at neck edge.

BO all sts kwise with WS facing.

Right Front Edging

With smaller needles, RS facing, and beg at lower edge of right front, pick up and knit 102 (110, 112) sts evenly spaced along right front edge to base of neck shaping.

ROW 1: (WS) Purl to last 6 sts, [k1, p1] 3 times.

ROW 2: (RS) Work 6 rib sts as they appear, purl to end.

ROW 3: Knit to last 6 sts, work 6 rib sts.

ROW 4: Work 6 rib sts, knit to end.

ROW 5: Purl to last 6 sts, work 6 rib sts.

Work short-rows to flare lower edge as foll:

NEXT ROW: (RS) Work 6 rib sts, k7, wrap next st, turn,

NEXT ROW: (WS) Purl to last 6 sts, work 6 rib sts.

NEXT ROW: (RS) Work 6 rib sts, knit to previously wrapped st, work wrap tog with wrapped st, k7, wrap next st, turn.

Rep the last 2 rows 9 (10, 11) more times—wrapped st in last RS row is the 88 (96, 104)th St st and 94 (102, 110)th st from beg of row.

NEXT ROW: (RS) Work 6 rib sts, knit to end.

NEXT ROW: (WS) Knit to last 6 sts, work 6 rib sts—edging measures 4¾ (5, 5¼)" (12 [12.5, 13.5] cm) from pick-up row at lower edge (the edge with ribbing) and 1" (2.5 cm) at neck edge.

BO all sts pwise with RS facing.

Neckband

With smaller needles, RS facing, and beg at the right front edging BO, pick up and knit 56 (70, 84) sts evenly spaced around neck edge, ending at the left front edging BO.

Purl 1 WS row.

Work 10 rows double garter st, ending with Row 2 of patt—neckband measures about 1¾" (4.5 cm) from pick-up row.

BO all sts.

Gently steam-block again, if desired.

For this classic jacket, I aimed for simple geometric shapes that would be fun to knit. The garter-stitch section of each front is super-easy, then fun is added as the corner is turned and stitches are picked up along the bottom edge for the cable pattern for the center fronts. Diverging increases shape the rounded lower front corners. A reverse-stockinette welt provides a firm foundation for a sleek zipper closure, while the slit pockets and stand-up collar complete the casual look.

FELIX

FINISHED SIZE

41 (44, 48, 51, 55)" (104 [112, 122, 129.5, 139.5] cm) bust/chest circumference, zipped.

Sweater shown measures 41" (104 cm).

YARN

Chunky weight (#5 Bulky).

Shown here: Berroco Cuzco (50% superfine alpaca, 50% Peruvian wool; 130 yd [119 m]/ 100 g): #9677 peat mix (dark green), 12 (13, 15, 16, 17) skeins.

NEEDLES

Body, sleeves, and edgings: size U.S. 9 (5.5 mm) straight and 32" (80 cm) circular (cir).

Pockets and collar: size U.S. 7 (4.5 mm).

Adjust needle size if necessary to obtain the correct gauge.

NOTIONS

Markers (m); 2 cable needles (cn); tapestry needle; 20 (21, 21, 22, 22)" (51 [54, 54, 56, 56] cm) separating zipper; sharp-point sewing needle and matching thread for inserting zipper.

GAUGE

16 sts and 32 rows = 4" (10 cm) in garter st on larger needles.

16 sts and 21 rows = 4" (10 cm) in St st on larger needles.

18 rows of center back cable chart = 3" (7.5 cm) high on larger needles.

stitch guide

2/2/2 TRIPLE CROSS

Slip 2 sts onto the first cn and hold in back of work, slip next 2 sts onto second cn and hold in front of work, k2, k2 from front cn, k2 from back cn.

notes

+ The back is worked sideways in one piece, beginning at the right side and ending at the left side. Each front is worked from the side toward the center of the body. The sleeves are worked from the upper edge down to the cuffs, then sewn into the armholes during finishing.

+ The center back cable pattern is deliberately not symmetrical at each side. There will be an X motif at the neck edge (beg of RS rows) and an O motif at the lower edge (end of RS rows).

+ The front edgings are worked along the lower and center front edges in one piece with increases to shape the front corners. The back edging is picked up and worked down from the back lower edge.

BACK

Right Side

With larger straight needles and using the long-tail method (see Glossary), CO 65 (67, 69, 69, 71) sts. Knit 10 (12, 14, 16, 18) rows, ending with a WS row—piece measures 1¼ (1½, 1¾, 2, 2¼)" (3.2 [3.8, 4.5, 5, 5.5] cm) from CO.

Right Armhole and Shoulder

With RS facing, use the cable method (see Glossary) to CO 30 (34, 38, 42, 42) sts, then knit across new sts, knit to end—95 (101, 107, 111, 113) sts total. Work even in garter st (knit every row) until shoulder measures 5½ (6, 6½, 7, 7½)" (14 [15, 16.5, 18, 19] cm) from sts CO for armhole, ending with a WS row.

Shape Back Neck

NEXT ROW: (RS) BO 3 (5, 7, 9, 9) sts, knit to end— 92 (96, 100, 102, 104) sts rem.

Work 5 rows in garter st, dec 1 st at neck edge at beg of each of the 2 RS rows and ending with a WS row—90 (94, 98, 100, 102) sts rem.

NEXT ROW: (RS) P0 (4, 8, 10, 0), place marker (pm), work Row 1 of Center Back Cable chart (see page 125) over 90 (90, 90, 90, 102) sts, inc as shown in chart (see Notes).

Working any sts for your size on the neck side of cable in Rev St st (purl RS rows, knit WS rows), work Rows 2–18 of chart, ending with a WS row— chart section measures 3" (7.5 cm) high.

Change to garter st and knit 5 rows, inc 1 st at neck edge at beg of the last 2 RS rows and ending with a RS inc row—92 (96, 100, 102, 104) sts rem.

NEXT ROW: (WS) Knit to end, then use the cable method to CO 3 (5, 7, 9, 9) sts—95 (101, 107, 111, 113) sts; back neck measures 4½" (11.5 cm) from BO at start of neck shaping.

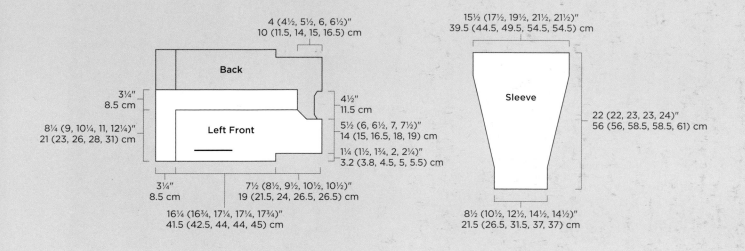

Back

Left Front

4 (4½, 5½, 6, 6½)"
10 (11.5, 14, 15, 16.5) cm

3¼"
8.5 cm

8¼ (9, 10¼, 11, 12¼)"
21 (23, 26, 28, 31) cm

4½"
11.5 cm

5½ (6, 6½, 7, 7½)"
14 (15, 16.5, 18, 19) cm

1¼ (1½, 1¾, 2, 2¼)"
3.2 (3.8, 4.5, 5, 5.5) cm

3¼"
8.5 cm

7½ (8½, 9½, 10½, 10½)"
19 (21.5, 24, 26.5, 26.5) cm

16¼ (16¾, 17¼, 17¼, 17¾)"
41.5 (42.5, 44, 44, 45) cm

Sleeve

15½ (17½, 19½, 21½, 21½)"
39.5 (44.5, 49.5, 54.5, 54.5) cm

22 (22, 23, 23, 24)"
56 (56, 58.5, 58.5, 61) cm

8½ (10½, 12½, 14½, 14½)"
21.5 (26.5, 31.5, 37, 37) cm

Left Armhole and Shoulder

Work even in garter st until shoulder measures 5½ (6, 6½, 7, 7½)" (14 [15, 16.5, 18, 19] cm) from sts CO at end of neck shaping, ending with a WS row.

NEXT ROW: (RS) BO 30 (34, 38, 42, 42) sts, knit to end—65 (67, 69, 69, 71) sts rem.

Left Side

Knit 10 (12, 14, 16, 18) rows, ending with a WS row—piece measures 1¼ (1½, 1¾, 2, 2¼)" (3.2 [3.8, 4.5, 5, 5.5] cm) from sts BO at armhole and 18 (19½, 21, 22½, 24)" (45.5 [49.5, 53.5, 57, 61] cm) from initial CO.

BO all sts evenly.

Back Edging

With larger needles and RS facing, pick up and knit 78 (86, 92, 98, 104) sts evenly along lower back edge.

SET-UP ROW: (WS) K2 (0, 3, 0, 3), [p2, k4] 12 (14, 14, 16, 16) times, p2, k2 (0, 3, 0, 3).

NEXT ROW: (RS) Establish patt from Row 1 of Back Edging Chart as foll, inc as shown on chart:

Work 2 (0, 3, 0, 3) sts in Rev St st (knit on RS rows, purl on WS rows), work 6 sts before patt rep box, work 12-st patt 5 (6, 6, 7, 7) times, work 8 sts after patt rep box, work 2 (0, 3, 0, 3) sts in Rev St st.

Working any sts at each side in Rev St st, work Rows 2–16 of chart. Work all sts in Rev St st for 10 rows, ending with a WS row.

Loosely BO all sts, leaving an 80" (203 cm) tail.

Fold last 10 rows in half with knit sides touching and purl sides facing out. With yarn threaded on a tapestry needle, sew BO edge to purl ridge of chart Row 16 on WS to form a heavy welt along

the outer edge—edging measures 3¼" (8.5 cm) from pick-up row to fold line.

RIGHT FRONT
Right Side

CO and work as for back right side, ending with a WS row—65 (67, 69, 69, 71) sts; piece measures 1¼ (1½, 1¾, 2, 2¼)" (3.2 [3.8, 4.5, 5, 5.5] cm) from CO.

Right Armhole, Pocket Opening, and Shoulder

NEXT ROW: (RS) Knit to end, then use the cable method to CO 30 (34, 38, 42, 42) sts—95 (101, 107, 111, 113) sts total.

Knit 3 rows, beg and ending with a WS row.

Work pocket opening on next 2 rows as foll:

NEXT ROW: (RS) K12 (14, 16, 16, 18), BO 25 sts, knit to end.

NEXT ROW: (WS) Knit to BO gap of previous row, use the cable method to CO 25 sts, knit to end.

Work even in garter st until shoulder measures 5½ (6, 6½, 7, 7½)" (14 [15, 16.5, 18, 19] cm) from sts CO for armhole, ending with a RS row.

Shape Front Neck

NEXT ROW: (WS) BO 10 (12, 14, 16, 16) sts, knit to end—85 (89, 93, 95, 97) sts rem.

DEC ROW: (RS) Knit to last 3 sts, k2tog, k1—1 st dec'd.

Work 1 WS row even. Rep the last 2 rows 5 (5, 7, 7, 9) more times, ending with a WS row—79 (83, 85, 87, 87) sts rem; front neck measures 1½ (1½, 2, 2, 2½)" (3.8, [3.8, 5, 5, 6.5] cm) from sts BO at start of shaping; piece measures 8¼ (9, 10¼, 11, 12¼)" (21 [23, 26, 28, 31] cm) from initial CO.

Cut yarn but leave sts on needle.

Right Front Edging

With RS facing, rejoin yarn to lower side edge of right front. With cir needle, pick up and knit 32 (38, 38, 44, 44) sts evenly along lower edge of front, pick up and knit 2 sts in corner, k79 (83, 85, 87, 87) sts on needle and inc 1 st as you work these sts—114 (124, 126, 134, 134) sts total.

SET-UP ROW: (WS) K0 (4, 0, 2, 2), [p2, k4] 13 (13, 14, 14, 14) times, p2, place marker (pm), p2 (corner sts), pm, p2, [k4, p2] 5 (6, 6, 7, 7) times.

NEXT ROW: (RS) Establish patt from Row 1 of Front Edging chart as foll, beg and ending where indicated for your size and inc as shown on chart: Work 6 (0, 0, 6, 6) sts before first patt rep box, work 12-st patt 2 (3, 3, 3, 3) times, work 2 sts after first patt rep box, slip marker (sl m), [k1f&b (see Glossary)] 2 times in corner sts as shown, sl m, work 2 sts before second patt rep box, work 12-st patt 6 (6, 7, 7, 7) times, work 6 (6, 0, 0,

0) sts after second patt rep box, work 0 (4, 0, 2, 2) sts in Rev St st.

Working any sts at neck edge for your size in Rev St st, work Rows 2–16 of chart—126 (136, 138, 146, 146) sts total; 14 sts between m at corner. Work all sts in Rev St st for 10 rows, ending with a WS row.

Loosely BO all sts, leaving a 40" (101.5 cm) tail.

Sew Rev St st welt as for back—edging measures 3¼" (8.5 cm) from pick-up row to fold line; piece measures 11½ (12¼, 13½, 14¼, 15½)" (29 [31, 34.5, 36, 39.5] cm) from initial CO to fold line.

LEFT FRONT
Left Side

CO and work as for back right side, ending with a WS row—65 (67, 69, 69, 71) sts; piece measures 1¼ (1½, 1¾, 2, 2¼)" (3.2 [3.8, 4.5, 5, 5.5] cm) from CO.

☐ knit on RS; purl on WS	＼ ssk	2/2RPC: sl 2 sts onto cn and hold in back, k2, p2 from cn
• purl on RS; knit on WS	▨ no stitch	2/2LPC: sl 2 sts onto cn and hold in front, p2, k2 from cn
M M1 (see Glossary)	☐ pattern repeat	2/2/2 triple cross (see Stitch Guide)
MP M1P (see Glossary)	❘ marker position	
／ k2tog	☑ k1f&b (see Glossary)	

Center Back Cable

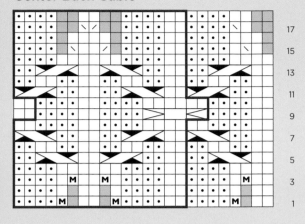

Back Edging

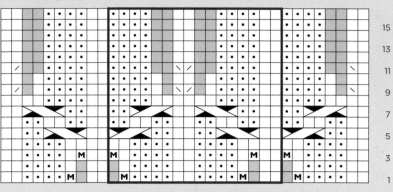

Front Edging

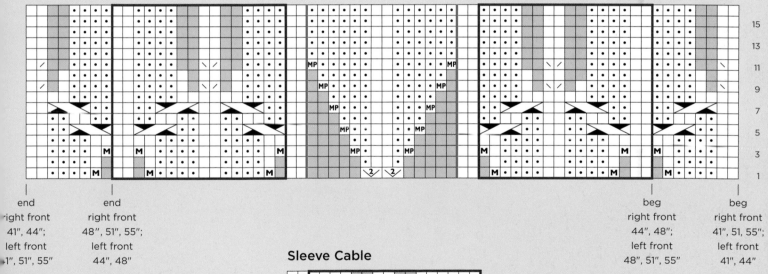

end
right front
41", 44";
left front
1", 51", 55"

end
right front
48", 51", 55";
left front
44", 48"

beg
right front
44", 48";
left front
48", 51", 55"

beg
right front
41", 51, 55";
left front
41", 44"

Sleeve Cable

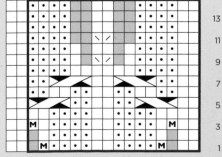

Left Armhole, Pocket Opening, and Shoulder

NEXT ROW: (RS) Use the cable method to CO 30 (34, 38, 42, 42) sts at beg of row, knit across new sts, knit to end—95 (101, 107, 111, 113) sts total.

Knit 3 rows, beg and ending with a WS row.

Work pocket opening on next 2 rows as foll:

NEXT ROW: (RS) K58 (62, 66, 70, 70), BO 25 sts, knit to end.

NEXT ROW: (WS) Knit to BO gap of previous row, use the cable method to CO 25 sts, knit to end.

Work even in garter st until shoulder measures 5½ (6, 6½, 7, 7½)" (14 [15, 16.5, 18, 19] cm) from sts CO for armhole, or 1 row less than for right front shoulder ending with a WS row.

Shape Front Neck

NEXT ROW: (RS) BO 10 (12, 14, 16, 16) sts, knit to end—85 (89, 93, 95, 97) sts rem.

Knit 1 WS row.

DEC ROW: (RS) K1, ssk, knit to end— 1 st dec'd.

Work 1 WS row even.

Rep the last 2 rows 5 (5, 7, 7, 9) more times, ending with a WS row—79 (83,

85, 87, 87) sts rem; front neck measures 1½ (1½, 2, 2, 2½)" (3.8, [3.8, 5, 5, 6.5] cm) from sts BO at start of shaping; piece measures 8¼ (9, 10¼, 11, 12¼)" (21 [23, 26, 28, 31] cm) from initial CO.

Left Front Edging

With RS facing and cir needle, k79 (83, 85, 87, 87) sts on needle and inc 1 st as you work them, pick up and knit 2 sts in corner, then pick up and knit 32 (38, 38, 44, 44) sts evenly along lower edge of front—114 (124, 126, 134, 134) sts total.

SET-UP ROW: (WS) [P2, k4] 5 (6, 6, 7, 7) times, p2, pm, p2 (corner sts), pm, p2, [k4, p2] 13 (13, 14, 14, 14) times, k0 (4, 0, 2, 2).

NEXT ROW: (RS) Establish patt from Row 1 of Front Edging chart as foll, beg and ending where indicated for your size and inc as shown on chart: Work 0 (4, 0, 2, 2) sts in Rev St st, work 6 (6, 0, 0, 0) sts before first patt rep box, work 12-st patt 6 (6, 7, 7, 7) times, work 2 sts after first patt rep box, sl m, [k1f&b] 2 times in corner sts as shown, sl m, work 2 sts before second patt rep box, work 12-st patt 2 (3, 3, 3, 3) times, work 6 (0, 0, 6, 6) sts after second patt rep box.

Working any sts at neck edge for your size in Rev St st, work Rows 2–16 of chart—126 (136, 138, 146, 146) sts total; 14 sts between m at corner. Work all sts in Rev St st for 10 rows, ending with a WS row.

Loosely BO all sts, leaving a 40" (101.5 cm) tail.

Sew Rev St st welt as for back—edging measures 3¼" (8.5 cm) from pick-up row to fold line; piece measures 11½ (12¼, 13½, 14¼, 15½)" (29 [31, 34.5, 36, 39.5] cm) from initial CO to fold line.

SLEEVES

With larger needles, CO 62 (70, 78, 86, 86) sts.

SET-UP ROW: (WS) K0 (4, 2, 0, 0), [p2, k4] 10 (10, 12, 14, 14) times, p2, k0 (4, 2, 0, 0).

NEXT ROW: (RS) Establish patt from Row 1 of Sleeve Cable chart as foll, inc as shown on chart:

Work 0 (4, 2, 0, 0) sts in Rev St st, work 12-st patt 5 (5, 6, 7, 7) times, work 2 sts after patt rep box, work 0 (4, 2, 0, 0) Rev St sts.

Working any sts at each side in Rev St st, work Rows 2–14 of chart. Knit 2 rows, then purl 2 rows, ending with a WS row—piece measures 2½" (6.5 cm) from CO.

Work 6 rows even in St st, ending with a WS row.

DEC ROW: (RS) K1, ssk, knit to last 3 sts, k2tog, k1—2 sts dec'd.

Work 5 rows even in St st.

Rep the shaping of the last 6 rows 12 more times, then rep the dec row once more—34 (42, 50, 58, 58) sts rem.

Work even in St st if necessary for your size until piece measures 18¾ (18¾, 19¾,19¾, 20¾)" (47.5 [47.5, 50, 50, 52.5] cm) from CO, ending with a WS row, or 3¼" (8.5 cm) less than desired length.

Cuff

ROW 1: (RS) K2, *p2, k2; rep from *.

ROW 2: (WS) P2, *k2, p2; rep from *.

Rep Rows 1 and 2 until cuff measures 2¾" (7 cm), ending with a RS row. Work all sts in Rev St st for 10 rows.

Loosely BO all sts, leaving an 18" (45.5 cm) tail.

Sew Rev St st welt as for back—edging measures 3¼" (8.5 cm) from pick-up row to fold line; sleeve measures 22 (22, 23, 23, 24)" (56 [56, 58.5, 58.5, 61] cm) from starting CO.

FINISHING

Weave in loose ends. Lightly steam-block pieces, taking care not to flatten texture patts.

Seams

With yarn threaded on a tapestry needle, sew fronts to back at shoulders. Sew sleeves into armholes. Sew sleeve and side seams.

Pockets

Pocket

With smaller needles and RS facing, pick up and knit 27 sts evenly spaced along BO edge of pocket opening closest to side seam (this is 2 sts more than the BO to allow 1 st at each side for seaming). Work even in St st for 5" (12.5 cm).

BO all sts.

Work the second pocket in the same manner.

Pocket Edging

With smaller needles and RS facing, pick up and knit 27 sts evenly spaced along CO edge of pocket slit (the edge closest to the center front).

NEXT ROW: (WS) P1, *k1, p1; rep from *.

Work sts as they appear for 5 more rows—edging measures about ¾" (2 cm).

BO all sts in rib patt.

Work a second edging in the same manner.

With yarn threaded on a tapestry needle, sew selvedges of each edging to RS of front as invisibly as possible. Sew three sides of each pocket firmly to WS of front.

Collar

With smaller needles and RS facing, pick up and knit 82 (86, 94, 98, 102) sts evenly spaced around neckline. Knit 1 WS row.

NEXT ROW: (RS) K2, *p2, k2; rep from *.

Work sts as they appear until collar measures 2½" (6.5 cm) from pick-up row.

Loosely BO all sts in rib.

Zipper

Position zipper with the top aligned with the collar pick-up row, the bottom aligned with the pick-up row of the lower front edging, and the front welts meeting in the center to conceal the zipper. With sharp-point sewing needle and thread, sew zipper in place (see Glossary).

The continuous cable pattern that frames the rounded edges of this vest is made possible through a series of short-rows. This piece begins with stitches cast on at the shoulders, then a series of increases and short-rows is worked—large sets that span the entire width of the work, followed by smaller sets that add swing to the cable edging and prevent it from curling. Add a pair of snug knit-two-purl-two sleeves, and you can turn this relaxed vest into a dressier bolero.

JACQUI

FINISHED SIZE
About 41 (44, 48, 51, 56)" (104 [112, 122, 129.5, 142] cm) bust circumference. Intended to be worn with 2" (5 cm) of positive ease.

Vest shown measures 41" (104 cm).

YARN
Worsted weight (#4 Medium).

Shown here: Berroco Blackstone Tweed (65% wool, 25% superkid mohair, 10% angora rabbit hair; 130 yd [119 m]/50 g): #2602 steamers, 5 (6, 7, 8, 9) balls.

NEEDLES
Body: size U.S. 7 (4.5 mm).

Armhole edging: size U.S. 6 (4 mm).

Adjust needle size if necessary to obtain the correct gauge.

NOTIONS
Markers (m); cable needle (cn); tapestry needle.

GAUGE
18 sts and 26½ rows = 4" (10 cm) in St st on larger needles.

20 sts in charted cable patts measure 3" (7.5 cm) wide on larger needles.

notes

+ The back is worked from side to side, beginning at the right side of the body and ending at the left side. The right and left fronts each start at the shoulder, continue down the front, and end at the side. Short-rows are used to shape the front armholes and lower edge curves.

+ Cable A is used for the right half of the back, then the direction of the cables reverses at center back by switching both the lower edge and collar cables to Cable B. In order for the cables to mirror one another in the center of the piece, the starting row for Cable B is determined by the last row worked for Cable A. If you ended Cable A with Row 6, begin Cable B with Row 1; if Cable A ended with Row 4, begin Cable B with Row 3; and if Cable A ended with Row 2, begin Cable B with Row 5.

+ When checking the length of the front edge, measure along the outer edge of the curve. You may find it helpful to use a flexible tape measure instead of a ruler.

BACK

Right Side

With larger needles, CO 54 (57, 60, 63, 66) sts.

SET-UP ROW: (WS) P2, place marker (pm), k2, p16, k2, pm, purl to end.

NEXT ROW: (RS) Knit to m, slip marker (sl m), work Row 1 of Cable A chart (see page 135) over 20 sts, sl m, k2.

Cont cable chart over 20 marked sts and working rem sts in St st, work even until piece measures 2 (2½, 2¾, 3¼, 3¾)" (5 [6.5, 7, 8.5, 9.5] cm) from CO, ending with a WS row.

Shape Right Armhole

Use the backward-loop method (see Glossary) to CO 2 sts at beg of next 3 RS rows, then CO 28 (29, 30, 31, 32) sts at beg of the foll RS row, working new sts in St st—88 (92, 96, 100, 104) sts. Work 1 WS row even—armhole shaping measures about 1¼" (3.2 cm) from first armhole CO row.

Shape Right Shoulder

INC ROW: (RS) K2, use the lifted method (see Glossary) to inc 1 st, knit to m, sl m, work in patt to end—1 st inc'd at shoulder.

Work 3 rows even.

Rep the last 4 rows 6 (6, 7, 7, 8) more times, ending with a WS row—95 (99, 104, 108, 113) sts; shoulder measures 4¼ (4¼, 4¾, 4¾, 5½)" (11 [11, 12, 12, 14] cm) from last CO row of armhole shaping; piece measures 7½ (8, 8¾, 9¼, 10½)" (19 [20.5, 22, 23.5, 26.5] cm) from initial CO.

Back Neck and Collar

NEXT ROW: (RS) Use the backward-loop method to CO 22 sts at beg of row for collar, work new sts as k2, pm, then work Row 1 of Cable A chart over 20 sts, pm, then work in established patt to end—117 (121, 126, 130, 135) sts.

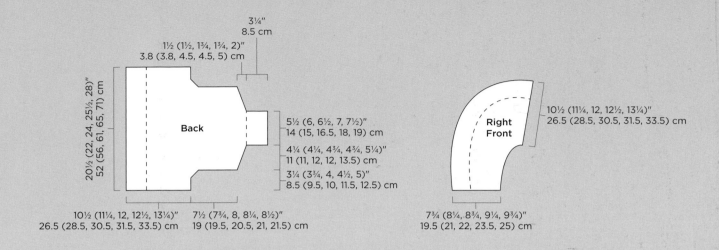

3¼"
8.5 cm

1½ (1½, 1¾, 1¾, 2)"
3.8 (3.8, 4.5, 4.5, 5) cm

20½ (22, 24, 25½, 28)"
52 (56, 61, 65, 71) cm

Back

5½ (6, 6½, 7, 7½)"
14 (15, 16.5, 18, 19) cm

4¼ (4¼, 4¾, 4¾, 5¼)"
11 (11, 12, 12, 13.5) cm

3¼ (3¾, 4, 4½, 5)"
8.5 (9.5, 10, 11.5, 12.5) cm

10½ (11¼, 12, 12½, 13¼)"
26.5 (28.5, 30.5, 31.5, 33.5) cm

7½ (7¾, 8, 8¼, 8½)"
19 (19.5, 20.5, 21, 21.5) cm

Right Front

10½ (11¼, 12, 12½, 13¼)"
26.5 (28.5, 30.5, 31.5, 33.5) cm

7¾ (8¼, 8¾, 9¼, 9¾)"
19.5 (21, 22, 23.5, 25) cm

NOTE: The cable patts at the lower edge and collar may not be on the same patt row; keep track of the cables individually, if necessary.

Cont cable patts as established over both groups of 20 marked sts, work rem sts in St st for 17 (19, 21, 23, 25) more rows, ending with a WS row—18 (20, 22, 24, 26) rows total in collar, back neck and collar measure 2¾ (3, 3¼, 3½, 3¾)" (7 [7.5, 8.5, 9, 9.5] cm).

On the next RS row, change to working both cable sections in patt from Cable B chart (see page 135), beg with the appropriate row (see Notes). Work even in patt until 18 (20, 22, 24, 26) rows of Cable B chart have been completed, ending with a WS row—back neck and collar measure 5½ (6, 6½, 7, 7½)" (14 [15, 16.5, 18, 19] cm).

NEXT ROW: (RS) BO 22 collar sts at beg of row, work in patt to end—95 (99, 104, 108, 113) sts rem.

Shape Left Shoulder

Work 1 WS row even.

DEC ROW: (RS) K2, ssk, knit to m, sl m, work in patt to end—1 st dec'd at shoulder.

Work 3 rows even.

Rep the last 4 rows 6 (6, 7, 7, 8) more times, ending with a WS row—88 (92, 96, 100, 104) sts; shoulder measures about 4¼ (4¼, 4¾, 4¾, 5¼)" (11 [11, 12, 12, 13.5] cm) from collar BO row; piece measures 17¼ (18¼, 20, 21, 23)" (44 [46.5, 51, 53.5, 58.5] cm) from initial CO.

Shape Left Armhole

BO 28 (29, 30, 31, 32) sts at beg of next RS row, then BO 2 sts at beg of foll 3 RS rows, ending with the last RS BO row—54 (57, 60, 63, 66) sts rem; armhole shaping measures about 1¼" (3.2 cm).

Left Side

Work even in patt until piece measures 2 (2½, 2¾, 3¼, 3¾)" (5 [6.5, 7, 8.5, 9.5] cm) from last armhole BO row and 20½ (22, 24, 25½, 28)" (52 [56, 61, 65, 71] cm) overall from initial CO.

BO all sts.

RIGHT FRONT

With larger needles, CO 42 (44, 46, 48, 50) sts.

SET-UP ROW: (WS) P2, pm, k2, p16, k2, pm, purl to end.

ROW 1: (RS) Knit to m, sl m, work Row 1 of Cable A chart over 20 sts, sl m, k2.

ROWS 2–5: Cont cable patt over 20 marked sts, work rem sts in St st for 4 more rows, ending with a RS row.

Work short-rows (see Glossary) to shape shoulder slope on Rows 6–9 as foll:

ROW 6: (WS) P2, sl m, work 20 sts in cable patt, sl m, wrap next st, turn.

ROWS 7 AND 9: Work in patt to end.

ROW 8: P2, sl m, work 20 sts in cable patt, sl m, work wrap tog with previous wrapped st, wrap next st, turn.

ROW 10: Work in patt across all sts, working wrap tog with wrapped st.

Work even in patt until piece measures 3½ (3¾, 4, 4¼, 4½)" (9 [9.5, 10, 11, 11.5] cm) along front edge (end of RS rows) and about ½" (1.3 cm) less at armhole edge (beg of RS rows), ending with a WS row.

Shape Armhole

INC ROW: (RS) K2, use the lifted method to inc 1 st, knit to m, sl m, work 20 cable sts, sl m, k2—1 st inc'd at armhole edge.

Work 3 rows even.

Rep the last 4 rows 1 (2, 3, 4, 5) more time(s), then work inc row once more, then work 2 rows even, ending with a RS row—45 (48, 51, 54, 57) sts total; 2 St sts at front edge; 20 cable sts; 23 (26, 29, 32, 35) St sts on armhole side of cable.

Work short-rows as foll:

ROW 1: (WS) P2, sl m, work 20 cable sts, sl m, wrap next st, turn.

ROWS 2 AND 4: (RS) Work in patt to end.

ROW 3: P2, sl m, work 20 cable sts, sl m, work wrap tog with previous wrapped st, p3, wrap next st, turn.

ROW 5: P2, sl m, work 20 cable sts, sl m, purl to wrapped st, work wrap tog with wrapped st, p2, wrap next st, turn.

ROW 6: Work in patt to end.

Rep the last 2 rows 4 (5, 6, 7, 8) more times, ending with a RS row—piece measures about 7¼ (8½, 9½, 10¾, 11¾)" (18.5 [21.5, 24, 27.5, 30] cm) from initial CO along front edge.

First Outer Cable Curve

Work a set of short-rows within the cable panel as foll:

ROW 1: (WS) P2, sl m, work first 18 sts of cable patt, wrap next st, turn.

ROW 2: (RS) Work in patt to end.

ROW 3: P2, sl m, work 18 sts in cable patt, work wrap tog with previous wrapped st, wrap next st (last st of cable), turn.

ROW 4: Work in patt to end.

Work 3 (5, 5, 7, 7) rows even in patt across all sts, working rem wrap tog with wrapped st in first row and ending with a WS row—piece measures 8¼ (9¾, 10¾, 12½, 13½)" (21 [25, 27.5, 31.5, 34.5] cm) along front edge from initial CO.

First Front Shaping

Work short-rows while increasing front inside cable panel as foll:

ROW 1: (RS) Knit to 1 st before m, use the lifted method to inc 1 st, knit to m, sl m, work in patt to end—46 (49, 52, 55, 58) sts total; 2 St sts at front edge; 20 cable sts; 24 (27, 30, 33, 36) St sts on armhole side of cable.

ROW 2: (WS) P2, sl m, work 20 cable sts, sl m, wrap next st, turn.

ROW 3: Work in patt to end.

ROW 4: P2, sl m, work 20 cable sts, sl m, work wrap tog with wrapped st, p3, wrap next st, turn.

ROW 5: Knit to 1 st before m, use the lifted method to inc 1 st, knit to m, sl m, work in patt to end—1 st inc'd.

ROW 6: P2, sl m, work 20 cable sts, sl m, purl to wrapped st, work wrap tog with wrapped st, p3, wrap next st, turn.

ROW 7: Work in patt to end.

ROW 8: Rep Row 6.

Rep Rows 5–8 of shaping 1 (1, 2, 2, 2) more time(s), then work Row 5 (Rows 5–7, Row 5, Rows 5–7, Rows 5–7) once more, ending with a RS row—49 (52, 56, 59, 62) sts total; 2 St sts at front edge; 20 cable sts; 27 (30, 34, 37, 40) St sts on armhole side of cable.

Work 3 (1, 3, 1, 1) row(s) even across all sts, working rem wrap tog with wrapped st in first row, and ending with a WS row.

Cont working across all sts, inc 1 st as before on next RS row, then work 1 WS row—50 (53, 57, 60, 63) sts total; 2 St sts at front edge; 20 cable sts; 28 (31, 35, 38, 41) St sts on armhole side of cable; piece measures 11 (12½, 14, 15¾, 16¾)" (28 [31.5, 35.5, 40, 42.5] cm) along front edge from initial CO.

Second Outer Cable Curve

Work as for first outer cable curve (see above), beg and ending with a WS row—no change to st counts; piece measures 12 (13¾, 15¼, 17½, 18½)" (30.5 [35, 38.5, 44.5, 47] cm) along front edge from initial CO.

Second Front Shaping

Work short-rows while increasing front inside cable panel as foll:

ROW 1: (RS) Knit to 1 st before m, use the lifted method to inc 1 st, knit to m, sl m, work in patt to end—51 (54, 58, 61, 64) sts total; 2 St sts at front edge; 20 cable sts; 29 (32, 36, 39, 42) St sts on armhole side of cable.

ROW 2: (WS) P2, sl m, work 20 cable sts, sl m, wrap next st, turn.

ROW 3: Work in patt to end.

ROW 4: P2, sl m, work 20 cable sts, sl m, work wrap tog with wrapped st, p3, wrap next st, turn.

□ knit on RS; purl on WS

· purl on RS; knit on WS

⬒ 2/2RC: sl 2 sts onto cn and hold in back, k2, k2 from cn

⬒ 2/2LC: sl 2 sts onto cn and hold in front, k2, k2 from cn

Cable A

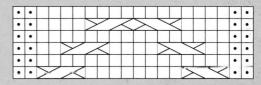

Cable B

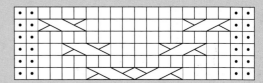

ROW 5: Knit to 1 st before m, use the lifted method to inc 1 st, knit to m, sl m, work in patt to end—1 st inc'd.

ROW 6: P2, sl m, work 20 cable sts, sl m, purl to wrapped st, work wrap tog with wrapped st, p3, wrap next st, turn.

ROW 7: Work in patt to end.

ROW 8: Rep Row 6.

Rep Rows 5–8 of shaping 2 (2, 1, 1, 1) more time(s)—54 (57, 60, 63, 66) sts total; 2 St sts at front edge; 20 cable sts; 32 (35, 38, 41, 44) St sts on armhole side of cable.

Without working any incs on RS rows, rep Rows 5–8 as before 0 (0, 1, 2, 2) more time(s).

Without working any incs, work Row 5 (Row 5, Rows 5–7, Row 5, Rows 5–7) once more, ending with a RS row—no change to st counts; piece measures 14½ (16¼, 18, 20¾, 22)" (37 [41.5, 45.5, 52.5, 56] cm) along front edge from initial CO.

Third Outer Cable Curve

Work as for first outer cable curve, beg and ending with a WS row—no change to st counts; piece measures 15½ (17½, 19¼, 22½, 23¾)" (39.5 [44.5, 49, 57, 60.5] cm) along front edge from initial CO.

Third Front Shaping

Work short-rows as foll:

ROWS 1 AND 3: (RS) Work in patt to end.

ROW 2: (WS) P2, sl m, work 20 cable sts, sl m, wrap next st, turn.

ROW 4: P2, sl m, work 20 cable sts, sl m, work wrap tog with wrapped st, p3, wrap next st, turn.

ROW 5: Work in patt to end.

ROW 6: P2, sl m, work 20 cable sts, sl m, purl to wrapped st, work wrap tog with wrapped st, p3, wrap next st, turn.

Rep the last 2 rows 5 (6, 7, 8, 8) more times, then work Row 5 once more, ending with a RS row—no change to st counts; piece measures 18 (20¼, 22½, 26, 27¼)" (45.5 [51.5, 57, 66, 69] cm) along front edge from initial CO.

Fourth and Fifth Outer Cable Curves and Front Shaping

For the fourth cable curve and fourth front shaping, *rep the third outer cable curve and third front shaping, then rep from * once more for the fifth cable curve and front shaping—piece measures about 25¼ (28¾, 31½, 36¼, 37½)" (64 [73, 80, 92, 95] cm) along front edge from initial CO.

Loosely BO all sts.

LEFT FRONT

With larger needles, CO 42 (44, 46, 48, 50) sts.

SET-UP ROW: (WS) P20 (22, 24, 26, 28), pm, k2, p16, k2, pm, p2.

ROW 1: (RS) K2, sl m, work Row 1 of Cable A chart over 20 sts, sl m, knit to end.

ROWS 2–6: Cont cable patt over 20 marked sts, work rem sts in St st for 5 more rows, ending with a WS row.

Work short-rows to shape shoulder slope on Rows 7–10 as foll:

ROW 7: (RS) K2, sl m, work 20 sts in cable patt, sl m, wrap next st, turn.

ROWS 8 AND 10: (WS) Work in patt to end.

ROW 9: K2, sl m, work 20 sts in cable patt, sl m, work wrap tog with previous wrapped st, wrap next st, turn.

ROW 11: Work in patt across all sts, working wrap tog with wrapped st.

Work even in patt until piece measures 3½ (3¾, 4, 4¼, 4½)" (9 [9.5, 10, 11, 11.5] cm) along front edge (beg of RS rows) and about ½" (1.3 cm) less at armhole edge (end of RS rows), ending with a WS row.

Shape Armhole

INC ROW: (RS) K2, sl m, work 20 cable sts, sl m, knit to last 2 sts, use the lifted method to inc 1 st, k2—1 st inc'd at armhole edge.

Work 3 rows even.

Rep the last 4 rows 1 (2, 3, 4, 5) more time(s), then work inc row once more, then work 1 WS row even—45 (48, 51, 54, 57) sts total; 2 St sts at front edge; 20 cable sts; 23 (26, 29, 32, 35) St sts on armhole side of cable.

Work short-rows as foll:

ROW 1: (RS) K2, sl m, work 20 cable sts, sl m, wrap next st, turn.

ROWS 2 AND 4: (WS) Work in patt to end.

ROW 3: K2, sl m, work 20 cable sts, sl m, work wrap tog with previous wrapped st, k3, wrap next st, turn.

ROW 5: K2, sl m, work 20 cable sts, sl m, knit to wrapped st, work wrap tog with wrapped st, k2, wrap next st, turn.

ROW 6: Work in patt to end.

Rep the last 2 rows 4 (5, 6, 7, 8) more times, ending with a WS row—piece measures about 7¼ (8½, 9½, 10¾, 11¾)" (18.5 [21.5, 24, 27.5, 30] cm) from initial CO along front edge.

First Outer Cable Curve

Work a set of short-rows within the cable panel as foll:

ROW 1: (RS) K2, sl m, work first 18 sts of cable patt, wrap next st, turn.

ROW 2: (WS) Work in patt to end.

ROW 3: K2, sl m, work 18 sts in cable patt, work wrap tog with previous wrapped st, wrap next st (last st of cable), turn.

ROW 4: Work in patt to end.

Work 2 (4, 4, 6, 6) rows even in patt across all sts, working rem wrap tog with wrapped st in first row, and ending with a WS row—piece measures 8¼ (9¾, 10¾, 12½, 13½)" (21 [25, 27.5, 31.5, 34.5] cm) along front edge from initial CO.

First Front Shaping

Work short-rows while increasing front inside cable panel as foll:

ROW 1: (RS) K2, sl m, work 20 cable sts, sl m, k1, use the lifted method to inc 1 st, knit to end—46 (49, 52, 55, 58) sts total; 2 St sts at front edge; 20 cable sts; 24 (27, 30, 33, 36) St sts on armhole side of cable.

ROWS 2, 4, AND 6: (WS) Work in patt to end.

ROW 3: K2, sl m, work 20 cable sts, sl m, wrap next st, turn.

ROW 5: K2, sl m, work 20 cable sts, sl m, work wrap tog with wrapped st, use the lifted method to inc 1 st, knit until there are 3 sts after m, wrap next st, turn—1 st inc'd.

ROW 7: K2, sl m, work 20 cable sts, sl m, knit to wrapped st, work wrap tog with wrapped st, k3, wrap next st, turn.

ROWS 8 AND 10: Work in patt to end.

ROW 9: K2, sl m, work 20 cable sts, sl m, k1, use the lifted method to inc 1 st, knit to wrapped st, work wrap tog with wrapped st, k3, wrap next st, turn—1 st inc'd.

Rep Rows 7–10 of shaping 0 (1, 1, 2, 2) more time(s), then work Rows 7–9 (Row 7, Rows 7–9, Row 7, Row 7) once more, ending with a RS row—49 (52, 56, 59, 62) sts total; 2 St sts at front edge; 20 cable sts; 27 (30, 34, 37, 40) St sts on armhole side of cable.

Work 3 (1, 3, 1, 1) row(s) even across all sts, working rem wrap tog with wrapped st in first row, and ending with a WS row.

Cont working across all sts, inc 1 st as before on next RS row, then work 1 WS row—50 (53, 57, 60, 63) sts total; 2 St sts at front edge; 20 cable sts; 28 (31, 35, 38, 41) St sts on armhole side of cable; piece measures 11 (12½, 14, 15¾, 16¾)" (28 [31.5, 35.5, 40, 42.5] cm) along front edge from initial CO.

Second Outer Cable Curve

Work as for first outer cable curve (see above), ending with a WS row—no change to st counts; piece measures 12 (13¾, 15¼, 17½, 18½)" (30.5 [35, 38.5, 44.5, 47] cm) along front edge from initial CO.

Second Front Shaping

Work short-rows while increasing front inside cable panel as foll:

ROW 1: (RS) K2, sl m, work 20 cable sts, sl m, k1, use the lifted method to inc 1 st, knit to end—51 (54, 58, 61, 64) sts total; 2 St sts at front edge; 20 cable sts; 29 (32, 36, 39, 42) St sts on armhole side of cable.

ROWS 2, 4, AND 6: (WS) Work in patt to end.

ROW 3: K2, sl m, work 20 cable sts, sl m, wrap next st, turn.

ROW 5: K2, sl m, work 20 cable sts, sl m, work wrap tog with wrapped st, use the lifted method to inc 1 st, knit until there are 3 sts after m, wrap next st, turn—1 st inc'd.

ROW 7: K2, sl m, work 20 cable sts, sl m, knit to wrapped st, work wrap tog with wrapped st, k3, wrap next st, turn.

ROWS 8 AND 10: Work in patt to end.

ROW 9: K2, sl m, work 20 cable sts, sl m, k1, use the lifted method to inc 1 st, knit to wrapped st, work wrap tog with wrapped st, k3, wrap next st, turn—1 st inc'd.

Rep Rows 7–10 of shaping 1 (1, 0, 0, 0) more time(s)—54 (57, 60, 63, 66) sts total; 2 St sts at front edge; 20 cable sts; 32 (35, 38, 41, 44) St sts on armhole side of cable.

Without working any incs on RS rows, rep Rows 7–10 as before 0 (0, 2, 2, 3) more times.

Without working any incs, work 4 (4, 2, 4, 2) rows even, ending with a WS row— no change to st counts; piece measures 14½ (16¼, 18, 20¾, 22)" (37 [41.5, 45.5, 52.5, 56] cm) along front edge from initial CO.

Third Outer Cable Curve

Work as for first outer cable curve, ending with a WS row—no change to st counts; piece measures 15½ (17½, 19¼, 22½, 23¾)" (39.5 [44.5, 49, 57, 60.5] cm) along front edge from initial CO.

Third Front Shaping

Work short-rows as foll:

ROW 1: (RS) K2, sl m, work 20 cable sts, sl m, wrap next st, turn.

ROWS 2 AND 4: (WS) Work in patt to end.

ROW 3: K2, sl m, work 20 cable sts, sl m, work wrap tog with wrapped st, k3, wrap next st, turn.

ROW 5: K2, sl m, work 20 cable sts, sl m, knit to wrapped st, work wrap tog with wrapped st, k3, wrap next st, turn.

ROW 6: Work in patt to end.

Rep the last 2 rows 5 (6, 7, 8, 8) more times, ending with a WS row—no change to st counts; piece measures 18 (20¼, 22½, 26, 27¼)" (45.5 [51.5, 57, 66, 69] cm) along front edge from initial CO.

Fourth and Fifth Outer Cable Curves and Front Shaping

For the fourth cable curve and fourth front shaping, *rep the third outer cable curve and third front shaping, then rep from * once more for the fifth cable curve and front shaping—piece measures about 25¼ (28¾, 31½, 36¼, 37½)" (64 [73, 80, 92, 95] cm) along front edge from initial CO.

Loosely BO all sts.

FINISHING

Weave in loose ends. Lightly steam-block pieces to measurements, taking care not to flatten cables.

With yarn threaded on a tapestry needle, sew shoulder seams.

Armhole Edgings

With smaller needles, RS facing, and beg at base of armhole, pick up and knit 90 (98, 106, 114, 122) sts evenly spaced around armhole opening. Purl 1 WS row, purl 1 RS row, then knit 2 rows.

BO all sts purlwise on next WS row.

Sew side seams.

Including influences from Aran patterns I saw in Ireland and techniques from Elizabeth Zimmermann, this jacket begins at the sleeve. The curved cap is shaped with internal increases, then the fun really begins at the yoke as the shoulder is shaped with more increases and the neck is shaped with short-rows. The shaping is reversed with decreases to the base of the other sleeve. Finally, stitches are picked up from the lower edge of the yoke and the body is worked quickly and easily to the hem.

JOSE

FINISHED SIZE

37½ (41½, 44¾, 47¾, 51½)" (95 [105.5, 113.5, 121.5, 131] cm) bust circumference, with 2¼" (5.5 cm) front bands overlapped.

Sweater shown measures 37½" (95 cm).

YARN

Worsted weight (#4 Medium).

Shown here: Lion Brand Fisherman's Wool (100% wool; 465 yd [425 m]/8 oz [227 g]): #150-123 oatmeal, 3 (4, 4, 4, 5) skeins.

NEEDLES

Body and sleeves: size U.S. 8 (5 mm).

Cuffs, lower edging, collar, and front bands: size U.S. 6 (4 mm): straight and 24" or 32" (60 or 80 cm) circular (cir).

Adjust needle size if necessary to obtain the correct gauge.

NOTIONS

Markers (m); cable needle (cn); stitch holder; tapestry needle; seven ⅞" (2.2 cm) buttons.

GAUGE

19 sts and 26 rows = 4" (10 cm) in St st on larger needles.

28 sts of charted cable patt = 4¼" (11 cm) wide on larger needles.

notes

+ The sleeves and yoke are knitted sideways in one piece, beginning at the left cuff and ending at the right cuff. The lower back and fronts are picked up along the lower edges of the yoke and worked downward.

+ The second stitch of a k1f&b increase creates a "pip" on the right side of the fabric. In order for the "pips" to appear as if they are 2 stitches away from the cable panel in the left sleeve, the increase before the cable is worked over 3 stitches as k1f&b, k2, and the increase after the cable panel is worked over 2 stitches as k1, k1f&b. In the underarm increases at the start of the right sleeve, the "pips" are placed 1 stitch in from the edge by working the k1f&b in the first stitch to increase at the beginning of the row and by working the last 2 stitches as k1f&b, k1 at the end of the row.

+ The schematic for this project does not show the garment parts oriented in the direction of the knitting.

SLEEVES AND YOKE

Left Sleeve

With smaller needles, CO 46 (46, 50, 50, 54) sts.

NEXT ROW: (RS) P2, *k2, p2; rep from *.

Work sts as they appear (knit the knits and purl the purls) until piece measures 3" (7.5 cm) from CO, ending with a RS row.

Change to larger needles.

NEXT ROW: (WS) Purl, inc 14 (16, 14, 16, 14) sts evenly spaced—60 (62, 64, 66, 68) sts.

NEXT ROW: (RS) Work 16 (17, 18, 19, 20) sts in St st, place marker (pm), work Row 1 (13, 9, 5, 1) of Cable chart (see page 145) over center 28 sts, pm, work 16 (17, 18, 19, 20) sts in St st.

Working sts at each side in St st, cont cable patt as established for your size until 16 cable rows have been completed, ending with WS Row 16 (12, 8, 4, 16) of chart—piece measures 5½" (14 cm) from CO.

INC ROW: (RS; see Notes) Knit to 2 sts before m, k1f&b (see Glossary), k2, slip marker (sl m), cont cable patt over center 28 sts, sl m, k1, k1f&b, knit to end—2 sts inc'd.

Cont in patt, [work 3 rows even, then rep the inc row] 18 (19, 20, 21, 22) times, working new sts in St st, and ending with RS Row 9 of chart for all sizes—98 (102, 106, 110, 114) sts; piece measures 16¾ (17¼, 18, 18½, 19¼)" (42.5 [44, 45.5, 47, 49] cm) from CO measured straight up along a single column of sts (do not measure along diagonal shaping).

Cont to inc each side of cable panel every 4th row as established and *at the same time* dec at each side to prevent the sleeve from growing wider as foll:

NEXT 3 ROWS: Work 3 rows even in patt, beg and ending with a WS row.

NEXT ROW: (RS) K1, ssk, knit to 2 sts before m, k1f&b, k2, sl m, work 28 sts cable patt, sl m, k1, k1f&b, knit to last 3 sts, k2tog, k1—no change to st count.

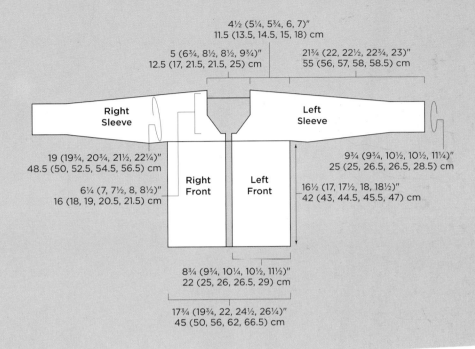

4½ (5¼, 5¾, 6, 7)"
11.5 (13.5, 14.5, 15, 18) cm

5 (6¾, 8½, 8½, 9¾)"
12.5 (17, 21.5, 21.5, 25) cm

21¾ (22, 22½, 22¾, 23)"
55 (56, 57, 58, 58.5) cm

Right Sleeve

Left Sleeve

19 (19¾, 20¾, 21½, 22¼)"
48.5 (50, 52.5, 54.5, 56.5) cm

6¼ (7, 7½, 8, 8½)"
16 (18, 19, 20.5, 21.5) cm

Right Front

Left Front

9¾ (9¾, 10½, 10½, 11¼)"
25 (25, 26.5, 26.5, 28.5) cm

16½ (17, 17½, 18, 18½)"
42 (43, 44.5, 45.5, 47) cm

8¾ (9¾, 10¼, 10½, 11½)"
22 (25, 26, 26.5, 29) cm

17¾ (19¾, 22, 24½, 26¼)"
45 (50, 56, 62, 66.5) cm

Rep the last 4 rows 5 (4, 4, 3, 3) more times, then work 1 (3, 1, 3, 1) row(s) even to end with WS Row 2 (16, 14, 12, 10) of chart.

Cont cable patt as established, work the sts at each side in alternating 2-row stripes of Rev St st and St st on next 6 rows as foll:

ROW 1: (RS) Purl to m, sl m, work 28 sts cable patt, sl m, purl to end.

ROWS 2 AND 3: Knit to m, sl m, work 28 sts cable patt, sl m, knit to end.

ROW 4: Rep Row 1.

ROWS 5 AND 6: Rep Rows 1 and 2 once more.

Working sts each side of center cable in St st, BO 7 sts at beg of next 2 rows,

ending with WS Row 10 (8, 6, 4, 2) of cable—84 (88, 92, 96, 100) sts rem; sleeve measures 21¾ (22, 22½, 22¾, 23)" (55 [56, 57, 58, 58.5] cm) from CO measured straight up along a single column of sts.

Left Shoulder

NOTE: The center cable continues as established to create a saddle shoulder while the stitches at each side are converted into a combination of cable and St st for the yoke.

NEXT ROW: (RS) Working Row 11 (9, 7, 5, 3) of chart over all cable panels, work first 28 sts in cable patt, pm if necessary for your size, work 0 (2, 4, 6, 8) St sts, sl m, work center 28 sts in cable patt,

sl m, work 0 (2, 4, 6, 8) St sts, pm if necessary for your size, work last 28 sts in cable patt.

Working any sts between cable panels in St st, work even for 1 (5, 9, 11, 17) row(s), ending with WS Row 12 (14, 16, 16, 4) of cable patt; shoulder measures ¼ (1, 1½, 1¾, 2¾)" (0.6 [2.5, 3.8, 4.5, 7] cm) from sts BO at end of sleeve.

INC ROW: (RS) Work 28 cable sts, sl m, knit any sts for your size to next m, M1 (see Glossary), sl m, work 28 cable sts, sl m, M1, knit any sts for your size to next m, sl m, work 28 cable sts—2 sts inc'd.

Working new sts in St st, [work 3 rows even in patt, then rep the inc row] 6 times, then work 3 rows even, ending

with WS Row 8 (10, 12, 12, 16) of cable patt—98 (102, 106, 110, 114) sts; 7 (9, 11, 13, 15) St sts on each side of center cable; shoulder measures 4½ (5¼, 5¾, 6, 7)" (11.5 [13.5, 14.5, 15, 18] cm) from sts BO at end of sleeve.

Left Front Neck

ROW 1: (RS; Row 9 [11, 13, 13, 1] of cables) Removing m on each side of center cable as you come to them, work in patt to center cable sts, work first 6 center cable sts as p2, k2, p2, BO rem 22 center cable sts, BO first 2 (3, 4, 5, 6) St sts, work in patt to end.

Place 41 (43, 45, 47, 49) back yoke sts before BO gap on holder to work later—33 (34, 35, 36, 37) front yoke sts rem on needle after BO gap.

NOTE: Cont the front cable patt as well as possible while working short-rows (see Glossary) to shape front neck; if there are not enough sts to work a complete cable crossing, work the cable sts in St st instead.

ROW 2: (WS) Work in patt to last 4 (6, 8, 10, 12) front sts, wrap next st, turn.

ROWS 3, 5, 7, 9, AND 11: (RS) Work in patt to end.

ROWS 4, 6, 8, 10, AND 12: Work in patt to 4 sts before previous wrapped st, wrap next st, turn—6 wrapped sts total; wrapped st in Row 12 is the 10 (9, 8, 7, 6)th st from beg of row.

ROW 13: (RS Row 5 [7, 9, 9, 13] of cable patt) Work in patt to end—front neck measures 2" (5 cm) from where back neck sts were placed on holder, measured along lower edge of yoke (end of RS rows).

Cont for your size as foll.

Size 37½" Only

With WS facing, BO all sts, working wraps tog with wrapped sts.

Sizes (41½, 44¾, 47¾, 51½)"

Cont in patt, work 1 WS row even, working wraps tog with wrapped sts.

BO (25, 27, 29, 31) sts at beg of next RS row—(9, 8, 7, 6) sts rem. Work (2, 6, 10, 10) rows even in patt, ending with RS Row (11, 1, 5, 9) of cable patt.

With WS facing, BO all sts.

All Sizes

Yoke measures 6½ (7¾, 9, 9¾, 10¾)" (16.5 [19.5, 23, 25, 27.5] cm) from sts BO at end of sleeve to sts BO at end of left front neck.

Back Neck

Return 41 (43, 45, 47, 49) held back yoke sts to needles and rejoin yarn with WS facing, ready to work a WS row. Beg with Row 10 (12, 14, 14, 2) of back cable and working rem sts of center cable in p2, k2 rib as established, work 32 (44, 56, 56, 64) rows even, ending with RS Row 9 (7, 5, 5, 1) of back cable—back neck measures 5 (6¾, 8½, 8½, 9¾)" (12.5 [17, 21.5, 21.5, 25] cm) from where back and front divided.

Place sts on holder.

Right Front Neck

Work for your size as foll.

Size 37½" Only

With larger needles, use the cable method (see Glossary) to CO 33 sts.

NEXT ROW: (RS) K5 for St st, pm, k18, work last 10 sts of chart Row 13 over last 10 sts of row.

Sizes (41½, 44¾, 47¾, 51½)"

With larger needles, use the cable method (see Glossary) to CO (9, 8, 7, 6) sts. Beg with RS Row (7, 1, 13, 9) of patt, work the last (9, 8, 7, 6) sts of the chart for (4, 8, 12, 12) rows, ending with WS Row (10, 8, 8, 4). With WS still facing, use the cable method to CO (25, 27, 29, 31) sts—(34, 35, 36, 37) sts.

NEXT ROW: (RS) K(6, 7, 8, 9) for St st, pm, k19 (20, 21, 22), work Row (11, 9, 9, 5) of cable patt over last (9, 8, 7, 6) sts.

All Sizes

Work short-rows as foll, working sts into established cable patt when they are first worked:

ROW 1: (WS; Row 14 [12, 10, 10, 6] of cable patt) Work 9 (8, 7, 6, 5) sts in patt, wrap the 10 (9, 8, 7, 6)th st, turn.

ROWS 2, 4, 6, 8, 10, AND 12: (RS) Work in patt to end.

ROWS 3, 5, 7, 9, AND 11: (WS) Work in patt to wrapped st, work wrap tog with wrapped st, work 3 sts in patt, wrap the next st (the 4th st after previously wrapped st), turn.

ROW 13: (WS; Row 10 [8, 6, 6, 2] of cable patt) Work in patt to end, working rem wrap tog with wrapped st, use the cable method to CO 24 (25, 26, 27, 28) sts at end of row for side of neck, return 41 (43, 45, 47, 49) held back yoke sts to needle with WS facing and work in patt across back sts—98 (102, 106, 110, 114)

sts total; lower edge of front yoke (end of RS rows) measures about 2 (2½, 3¼, 3¾, 3¾)" (5 [6.5, 8.5, 9.5, 9.5] cm) from sts CO at start of right front neck.

Right Shoulder

Re-establish patts with 28 cable sts at each side, 28 center cable sts, and 7 (9, 11, 13, 15) sts between cable panels. Work 2 rows even in patt, ending with WS Row 12 (10, 8, 8, 4) of cable patt.

DEC ROW: (RS) Work 28 cable sts, sl m, knit to 2 sts before next m, k2tog, sl m, work 28 cable sts, sl m, ssk, knit to next m, sl m, work 28 cable sts—2 sts dec'd.

NOTE: For the smallest size, when only 1 St st remains between the cables, purl the first rem St st tog with the last st of the back cable and purl the second rem St st tog with the first st of the front cable; do not work these St sts tog with the center cable.

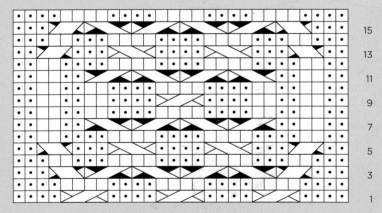

	knit on RS; purl on WS
•	purl on RS; knit on WS

2/1RPC: sl 1 st onto cn and hold in back, k2, p1 from cn

2/1LPC: sl 2 sts onto cn and hold in front, p1, k2 from cn

2/2RC: sl 2 sts onto cn and hold in back, k2, k2 from cn

2/2LC: sl 2 sts onto cn and hold in front, k2, k2 from cn

2/2RPC: sl 2 sts onto cn and hold in back, k2, p2 from cn

2/2LPC: sl 2 sts onto cn and hold in front, p2, k2 from cn

Cable

15
13
11
9
7
5
3
1

[Work 3 rows even in patt, then rep the dec row] 6 times, ending with RS Row 5 (3, 1, 1, 13) of cable patt—84 (88, 92, 96, 100) sts rem; 0 (2, 4, 6, 8) St sts rem between cable panels.

Work even for 2 (6, 10, 12, 18) rows, ending with RS Row 7 (9, 11, 13, 15) of cable patt; shoulder measures about 4½ (5¼, 5¾, 6, 7)" (11.5 [13.5, 14.5, 15, 18] cm) from sts CO at side of right neck shaping; yoke measures 14 (17¼, 20, 20½, 23¾)" (35.5 [44, 51, 52, 60.5] cm) from sts BO at end of left sleeve measured along back yoke edge (beg of RS rows).

Right Sleeve

Working all sts on each side of center cable in St st, use the cable method to CO 7 sts at beg of next 2 rows, ending with RS Row 9 (11, 13, 15, 1) of cable patt—98 (102, 106, 110, 114) sts.

Cont center cable patt as established, work the sts at each side in alternating 2-row stripes of Rev St st and St st on next 6 rows as foll:

ROW 1: (RS) Purl to m, sl m, work 28 sts cable patt, sl m, purl to end.

ROWS 2 AND 3: Knit to m, sl m, work 28 sts cable patt, sl m, knit to end.

ROW 4: Rep Row 1.

ROWS 5 AND 6: Rep Rows 1 and 2 once more.

Work 1 (3, 1, 3, 1) row(s) even to end with WS Row 16 (4, 4, 8, 8) of cable.

Beg dec on each side of cable panel every 4th row and *at the same time* inc at each side (see Notes) to prevent the sleeve from growing narrower as foll:

NEXT ROW: (RS) K1f&b, knit to 2 sts before m, ssk, sl m, work cable as established, sl m, k2tog, knit to last 2 sts, k1f&b, k1—no change to stitch count.

NEXT 3 ROWS: Work 3 rows even in patt, beg and ending with a WS row.

Rep the last 4 rows 5 (4, 4, 3, 3) more times, ending with WS Row 8 of cable patt for all sizes—piece measures 5 (4¾, 4½, 4¼, 3¾)" (12.5 [12, 11.5, 11, 9.5] cm) from sts CO at beg of sleeve.

Discontinue incs at sides, but cont to work decs on each side of cable panel every 4th row as foll:

DEC ROW: (RS) Knit to 2 sts before m, ssk, sl m, work cable as established, sl m, k2tog, knit to end—2 sts dec'd.

Cont in patt, [work 3 rows even, the rep the dec row] 18 (19, 20, 21, 22) times, ending with RS Row 1 (5, 9, 13, 1) of cable patt—60 (62, 64, 66, 68) sts rem. Work 16 rows even in patt, ending with RS Row 1 (5, 9, 13, 1) of cable patt again—piece measures 18¾ (19, 19½, 19¾, 20)" (47.5 [48.5, 49.5, 50, 51] cm) from sts CO at beg of sleeve.

NEXT ROW: (WS) Purl, dec 14 (16, 14, 16, 14) sts evenly spaced—46 (46, 50, 50, 54) sts rem.

Change to smaller needles.

NEXT ROW: (RS) P2, *k2, p2; rep from *.

Work sts as they appear until ribbed cuff measure 3" (7.5 cm), ending with a WS row—piece measures 21¾ (22, 22½, 22¾, 23)" (55 [56, 57, 58, 58.5] cm)" from sts CO at beg of sleeve.

Loosely BO all sts in rib.

BACK

Mark the center of the back yoke edge. With larger needles and RS facing, pick up and knit 7 sts across sts BO at left underarm, 43 (48, 53, 59, 63) sts along back edge to center m, 43 (48, 53, 59, 63) sts from center to right sleeve, then knit 7 sts across sts CO at right underarm—100 (110, 120, 132, 140) sts total. Purl 1 WS row.

Work alternating 2-row stripes of Rev St st and St st on next 6 rows as foll:

ROW 1: (RS) Purl.

ROWS 2 AND 3: Knit.

ROW 4: Purl.

ROWS 5 AND 6: Rep Rows 1 and 2 once more.

NEXT ROW: (RS) K12 (15, 18, 22, 24), pm, work Row 1 of cable chart over 28 sts, pm, k20 (24, 28, 32, 36) center sts, pm, work Row 1 cable chart over 28 sts, pm, k12 (15, 18, 22, 24).

Working sts outside cable panels in St st, cont in established patts until back measures 14½ (15, 15½, 16, 16½)" (37 [38, 39.5, 40.5, 42] cm) from pick-up row, ending with a WS row and *at the same time* dec 1 (0, 1, 1, 1) st at each end of last row—98 (110, 118, 130, 138) sts.

Change to smaller needles.

NEXT ROW: (RS) P2, *k2, p2; rep from *.

Work sts as they appear until rib measures 2" (5 cm)—back measures 16½ (17, 17½, 18, 18½)" (42 [43, 44.5, 45.5, 47] cm) from pick-up row.

Loosely BO all sts in rib.

LEFT FRONT

With larger needles and RS facing, pick up and knit 43 (47, 49, 51, 55) sts along left front yoke edge, then 7 sts across BO sts at left underarm—50 (54, 56, 58, 62) sts total. Purl 1 WS row, then work alternating 2-row stripes of Rev St st and St st on next 6 rows as for back.

NEXT ROW: (RS) K11 (13, 14, 15, 17), pm, work Row 1 of cable chart over center 28 sts, pm, k11 (13, 14, 15, 17).

Working sts outside cable panel in St st, cont in established patts until front measures 14½ (15, 15½, 16, 16½)" (37 [38, 39.5, 40.5, 42] cm) from pick-up row, ending with a WS row and *at the same time* dec 0 (0, 1, 0, 0) st at each end of last row—50 (54, 54, 58, 62) sts.

Change to smaller needles.

Work rib patt as for back—front measures 16½ (17, 17½, 18, 18½)" (42 [43, 44.5, 45.5, 47] cm) from pick-up row.

Loosely BO all sts in rib.

RIGHT FRONT

With larger needles and RS facing, pick up and knit 7 sts across sts CO at right underarm, then 43 (47, 49, 51, 55) sts along right front yoke edge—50 (54, 56, 58, 62) sts total. Complete as for left front.

FINISHING

Weave in loose ends. Lightly steam-block pieces, taking care not to flatten texture patts. With yarn threaded on a tapestry needle, sew sleeve and side seams.

Front Bands and Collar

With smaller cir needle, RS facing, and beg at lower right front corner, pick up and knit 74 (76, 78, 80, 82) sts evenly spaced to end at Row 6 of the Rev St st stripes (bottom edge of bottom stripe), 60 (66, 72, 74, 76) sts along right front neck, pm, 22 (30, 38, 38, 42) sts across back neck, pm, 60 (66, 72, 74, 76) sts along left front neck to end at Row 6 of Rev St st stripes (bottom edge of bottom stripe), and 74 (76, 78, 80, 82) sts along left front to lower corner—290 (314, 338, 346, 358) sts total.

NEXT ROW: (WS) K2, *p2, k2; rep from *—with RS facing, sts at each end of marked back neck section should be k2.

Work sts as they appear for 6 more rows, ending with a WS row.

Shape Collar

Work short-rows to raise back neck for shawl collar while inc on each side of back neck section as foll:

ROW 1: (RS) Work 209 (231, 253, 259, 269) sts in patt to 7 sts before end of left neck sts, wrap next st, turn.

ROW 2: (WS) Work 128 (148, 168, 172, 180) sts in patt to 7 sts before end of right neck sts, wrap next st, turn.

ROW 3: Work in patt to first back neck m, sl m, M1, k2, M1, work in patt to 2 sts before second back neck m, M1, k2, M1, sl m, work in patt to 4 sts before previously wrapped st, wrap next st, turn—4 sts inc'd.

ROW 4: Work in patt to first back neck m, sl m, p4, work in patt to 4 sts before second back neck m, p4, sl m, work in patt to 4 sts before previously wrapped st, wrap next st, turn.

ROWS 5 AND 6: Work sts as they appear to 4 sts before previously wrapped st, wrap next st, turn.

ROW 7: Work in patt to first back neck m, sl m, *k1, work [k1, p1] in next st, work [p1, k1] in foll st, k1,* work in patt to 4 sts before second back neck m, rep from * to *, sl m, work in patt to 4 sts before previously wrapped st, wrap next st, turn—4 sts inc'd.

ROWS 8–10: Working back section in established k2, p2 rib, work in patt to 4 sts before previously wrapped st, wrap next st, turn.

ROW 11: Work in patt to first back neck m, sl m, *k2, p1f&b (see Glossary) in each of next 2 sts, k2,* work in patt to 6 sts before second back neck m, rep from * to *, sl m, work in patt to 4 sts before previously wrapped st, wrap next st, turn—4 sts inc'd.

ROW 12: Work in patt to first back neck m, sl m, p2, k4, p2, work in patt to 8 sts before second back neck m, p2, k4, p2, sl m, work in patt to 4 sts before previously wrapped st, wrap next st, turn.

ROWS 13 AND 14: Work sts as they appear to 4 sts before previously wrapped st, wrap next st, turn.

ROW 15: Work in patt to first back neck m, sl m, *k2, p1, work [p1, k1] in next st, work [k1, p1] in foll st, p1, k2,* work in patt to 8 sts before second back neck m, rep from * to *, sl m, work in patt to 4 sts before previously wrapped st, wrap next st, turn—4 sts inc'd; 306 (330, 354, 362, 374) sts total; 38 (46, 54, 54, 58) sts between back m.

ROW 16: Working back section in established k2, p2 rib, work in patt to 4 sts before previously wrapped st, wrap next st, turn—8 wrapped sts at each side.

Work in rib patt to end of needle for 2 rows, working wraps tog with wrapped sts as you come to them and ending with a WS row.

BUTTONHOLE ROW: (RS) Work 227 (249, 271, 277, 287) sts rib patt to 5 sts before end of left neck sts, [work 2 sts tog as k2tog or p2tog to maintain patt, yo, work 11 (11, 12, 12, 12) sts in rib patt] 5 times, work 2 sts tog, yo, work 6 (8, 5, 7, 9) sts in rib patt, work 2 sts tog, yo, work 4 sts in rib patt—7 buttonholes.

Work 6 rows even in rib patt—shawl collar measures 4½" (11.5 cm) from pick-up row at center back; front bands measure 2¼" (5.5 cm) from pick-up row along front edges.

Loosely BO all sts in patt.

Sew buttons to right front, opposite buttonholes.

GLOSSARY

ABBREVIATIONS

beg(s)	begin(s); beginning	**M1**	make one (increase)	**st(s)**	stitch(es)
BO	bind off	**p**	purl	**St st**	stockinette stitch
CC	contrasting color	**p1f&b**	purl into front and back of same stitch	**tbl**	through back loop
cm	centimeter(s)			**tog**	together
cn	cable needle	**patt(s)**	pattern(s)	**WS**	wrong side
CO	cast on	**psso**	pass slipped stitch over	**wyb**	with yarn in back
cont	continue(s); continuing	**pwise**	purlwise, as if to purl	**wyf**	with yarn in front
dec(s)	decrease(s); decreasing	**rem**	remain(s); remaining	**yd**	yard(s)
dpn	double-pointed needles	**rep**	repeat(s); repeating	**yo**	yarnover
foll	follow(s); following	**Rev St st**	reverse stockinette stitch	*	repeat starting point
g	gram(s)	**rnd(s)**	round(s)	* *	repeat all instructions between asterisks
inc(s)	increase(s); increasing	**RS**	right side		
k	knit	**sl**	slip	( )	alternate measurements and/ or instructions
k1f&b	knit into the front and back of same stitch	**sl st**	slip st (slip 1 stitch purlwise unless otherwise indicated)	[ ]	work instructions as a group a specified number of times
kwise	knitwise, as if to knit	**ssk**	slip 2 stitches knitwise, one at a time, from the left needle to right needle, insert left needle tip through both front loops and knit together from this position (1 stitch decrease)		
m	marker(s)				
MC	main color				
mm	millimeter(s)				

BIND-OFFS
Standard Bind-Off

Knit the first stitch, *knit the next stitch (2 stitches on right needle), insert left needle tip into first stitch on right needle **(Figure 1)** and lift this stitch up and over the second stitch **(Figure 2)** and off the needle **(Figure 3)**. Repeat from * for the desired number of stitches.

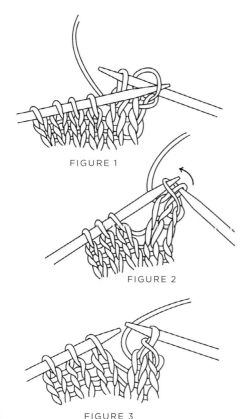

FIGURE 1

FIGURE 2

FIGURE 3

CABLES WITHOUT A CABLE NEEDLE

NOTE: The instructions here are for working a cable that involves just two stitches in which one stitch crosses the other. The same principles apply to cables worked over more stitches.

STEP 1: Slip the desired number of stitches (one stitch shown) off of the left-hand needle **(Figure 1)**, letting them drop temporarily in the front of the work for a right-leaning cable or in the back of the work for a left-leaning cable.

STEP 2: Slip the desired number of stitches (one stitch shown) temporarily onto the right-hand needle, keeping the dropped stitch(es) in front **(Figure 2)** or back of the work as established.

STEP 3: Return the dropped stitch(es) onto the left-hand needle, then return the held stitch(es) from the right-hand needle onto the left-hand needle **(Figure 3)** so that the two groups of stitches are reversed from their original order.

STEP 4: Knit the two groups of stitches in their new order **(Figure 4)**.

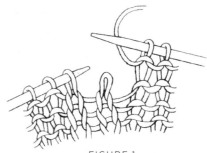

FIGURE 1

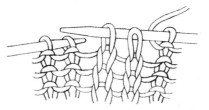

FIGURE 2

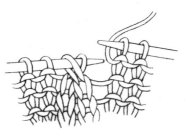

FIGURE 3

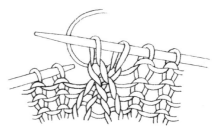

FIGURE 4

CAST-ONS

Backward-Loop Cast-On

*Loop working yarn and place it on needle backward so that it doesn't unwind. Repeat from *.

Cable Cast-On

If there are no stitches on the needles, make a slipknot of working yarn and place it on the needle, then use the knitted method (shown at right) to cast on one more stitch—2 stitches on needle. Hold needle with working yarn in your left hand with the wrong side of the work facing you. *Insert right needle between the first two stitches on left needle **(Figure 1)**, wrap yarn around needle as if to knit, draw yarn through **(Figure 2)**, and place new loop on left needle, twisting it as you do so **(Figure 3)**, to form a new stitch. Repeat from * for the desired number of stitches, always working between the first two stitches on the left needle.

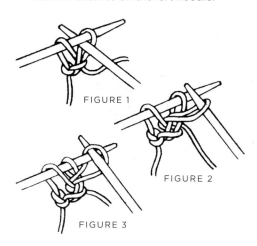

FIGURE 1

FIGURE 2

FIGURE 3

Knitted Cast-On

Make a slipknot and place it on the left needle if there are no stitches already there. *Use the right needle to knit the first stitch (or slipknot) on left needle **(Figure 1)** and place new loop onto left needle, twisting it as you do so, to form a new stitch **(Figure 2)**. Repeat from * for the desired number of stitches, always working into the last stitch made.

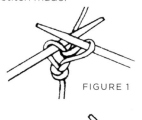

FIGURE 1

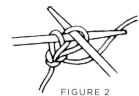

FIGURE 2

Long-Tail (Continental) Cast-On

Leaving a long tail (about ½″ [1.3 cm] for each stitch to be cast on), make a slipknot and place on right needle. Place thumb and index finger of your left hand between the yarn ends so that working yarn is around your index finger and tail end is around your thumb and secure the yarn ends with your other fingers. Hold your palm upwards, making a V of yarn **(Figure 1)**. *Bring needle up through loop on thumb **(Figure 2)**, catch first strand around index finger, and go back down through loop on thumb **(Figure 3)**. Drop loop off thumb and, placing thumb back in V configuration, tighten resulting stitch on needle **(Figure 4)**. Repeat from * for the desired number of stitches.

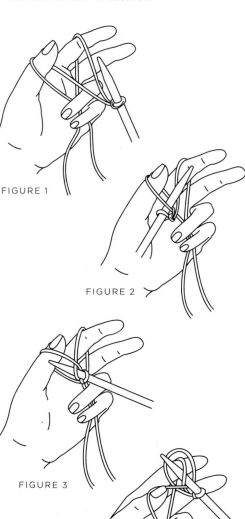

FIGURE 1

FIGURE 2

FIGURE 3

FIGURE 4

DECREASES

Slip, Slip, Knit (ssk)

Slip two stitches individually knitwise **(Figure 1)**, insert left needle tip into the front of these two slipped stitches, and use the right needle to knit them together through their back loops **(Figure 2)**.

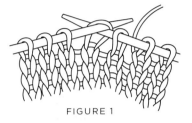

FIGURE 1

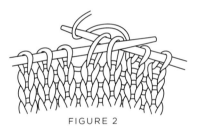

FIGURE 2

Slip, Slip, Slip, Knit (sssk)

This decrease is similar to the ssk method illustrated above, but involves three stitches instead of two.

Slip three stitches individually knitwise, insert left needle tip into the front of all three slipped stitches, and use the right needle to knit them together through their back loops.

Slip, Slip, Purl (ssp)

Holding yarn in front, slip two stitches individually knitwise **(Figure 1)**, then slip these two stitches back onto left needle (they will be twisted on the needle) and purl them together through their back loops **(Figure 2)**.

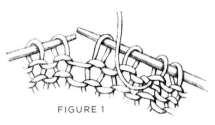

FIGURE 1

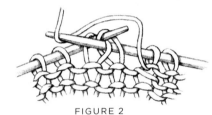

FIGURE 2

INCREASES

Knit in the Front and Back (k1f&b)

Knit into a stitch but leave it on the left needle **(Figure 1)**, then knit through the back loop of the same stitch **(Figure 2)** and slip the original stitch off the needle **(Figure 3)**.

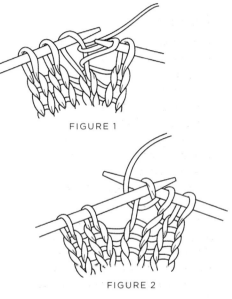

FIGURE 1

FIGURE 2

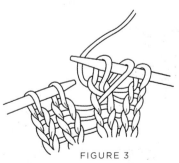

FIGURE 3

Lifted Increase

Knit into the back of the stitch (in the "purl bump") in the row directly below the stitch on the needle **(Figure 1)**, then knit the stitch on the needle and slip the original stitch off the needle **(Figure 2)**.

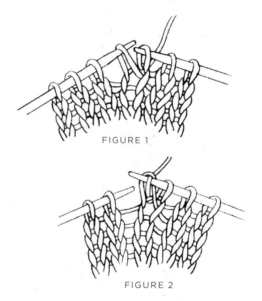

FIGURE 1

FIGURE 2

Make One (M1)

With left needle tip, lift the strand between the last knitted stitch and the first stitch on the left needle from front to back **(Figure 1)**, then knit the lifted loop through the back **(Figure 2)**.

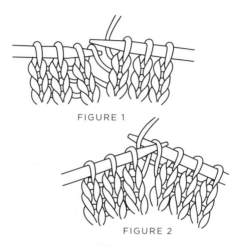

FIGURE 1

FIGURE 2

Make One Purlwise (M1P)

With left needle tip, lift the strand between the needles from front to back **(Figure 1)**, then purl the lifted loop through the back **(Figure 2)**.

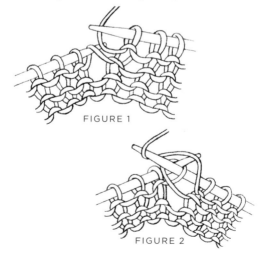

FIGURE 1

FIGURE 2

Purl in the Front and Back (p1f&b)

Purl into a stitch but leave the stitch on the left needle **(Figure 1)**, then purl through the back loop of the same stitch **(Figure 2)** and slip the original stitch off the needle.

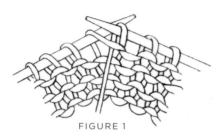

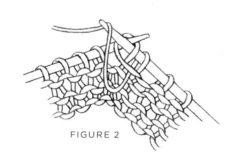

FIGURE 1

FIGURE 2

SEAMS

Mattress Stitch

Place the pieces to be seamed on a table, right sides facing up. Begin at the lower edge and work upward as follows for your stitch pattern:

Stockinette Stitch with 1-Stitch Seam Allowance

Insert threaded needle under one bar between the two edge stitches on one piece, then under the corresponding bar plus the bar above it on the other piece (Figure 1). *Pick up the next two bars on the first piece (Figure 2), then the next two bars on the other (Figure 3). Repeat from *, ending by picking up the last bar or pair of bars on the first piece.

Stockinette Stitch with ½-Stitch Seam Allowance

To reduce bulk in the mattress stitch seam, work as for the 1-stitch seam allowance but pick up the bars in the center of the edge stitches instead of between the last two stitches.

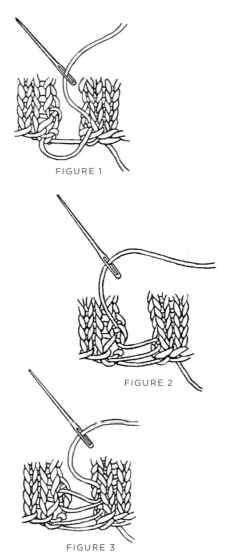

FIGURE 1

FIGURE 2

FIGURE 3

Slip-Stitch Crochet

To begin, place a slipknot on a crochet hook. With wrong side facing together and working one stitch as a time, *insert crochet hook through both thicknesses into the edge stitches (Figure 1), grab a loop of yarn and draw this loop through both thicknesses, then through the loop on the hook (Figure 2). Repeat from *.

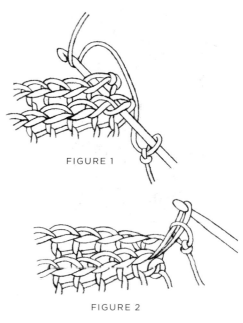

FIGURE 1

FIGURE 2

SHORT-ROWS

Short-Rows Knit Side

Work to the turning point, slip the next stitch purlwise **(Figure 1)**, bring the yarn to the front, then slip the same stitch back to the left needle **(Figure 2)**, turn the work around and bring the yarn in position for the next stitch—one stitch has been wrapped and the yarn is correctly positioned to work the next stitch.

When you come to a wrapped stitch on a subsequent row, hide the wrap by working it together with the wrapped stitch as follows: Insert right needle tip under the wrap (from the front if wrapped stitch is a knit stitch; from the back if the wrapped stitch is a purl stitch; **Figure 3**), then into the stitch on the needle, and work the stitch and its wrap together as a single stitch.

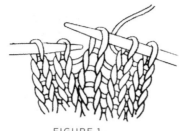

FIGURE 1

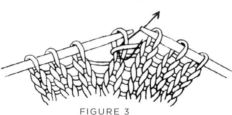

FIGURE 2

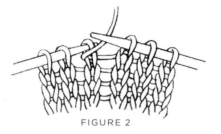

FIGURE 3

Short-Rows Purl Side

Work to the turning point, slip the next stitch purlwise to the right needle, bring the yarn to the back of the work **(Figure 1)**, return the slipped stitch to the left needle, bring the yarn to the front between the needles **(Figure 2)**, and turn the work so that the knit side is facing—one stitch has been wrapped and the yarn is correctly positioned to knit the next stitch.

To hide the wrap on a subsequent purl row, work to the wrapped stitch, use the tip of the right needle to pick up the wrap from the back, place it on the left needle **(Figure 3)**, then purl it together with the wrapped stitch.

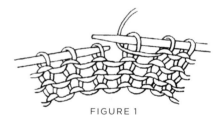

FIGURE 1

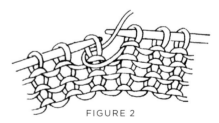

FIGURE 2

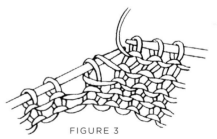

FIGURE 3

ZIPPER

With right side facing up and zipper closed, pin zipper to knitted pieces so that the edges of the knitting meet at the zipper teeth. With contrasting thread and right side facing, baste zipper in place close to the teeth **(Figure 1)**. Turn the work over and with matching sewing thread and needle, stitch the outer edges of the zipper to the wrong side of knitting **(Figure 2)**, being careful to follow a single column of stitches in the knitting to keep the zipper straight. Turn the work so the right side is facing again and with matching sewing thread, sew the knitted fabric close to the teeth **(Figure 3)**. Remove basting.

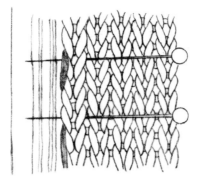

FIGURE 1

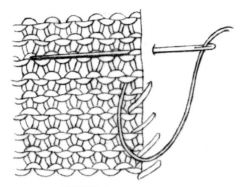

FIGURE 2

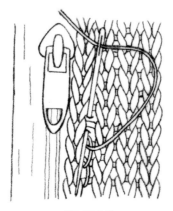

FIGURE 3

YARN SOURCES

Berroco Inc.
1 Tupperware Dr., Ste. 4
North Smithfield, RI 02896
berroco.com
in Canada: S. R. Kertzer Ltd.

Brown Sheep Company
100662 County Rd. 16
Mitchell, NE 69357
brownsheep.com

Cascade Yarns
PO Box 58168
1224 Andover Park E.
Tukwila, WA 98188
cascadeyarns.com

Classic Elite Yarns
122 Western Ave.
Lowell, MA 01851
classiceliteyarns.com

CNS Yarns/Mission Falls
100 Walnut, Door 4
Champlain, NY 12919
missionfalls.com
in Canada:
1050 8th St.
Grand-Mère, QC
Canada G9T 4L4

Diamond Yarn
9697 St. Laurent, Ste. 101
Montréal, QC
Canada H3L 2N1
and
155 Martin Ross, Unit 3
Toronto, ON
Canada M3J 2L9
diamondyarn.com

S. R. Kertzer Ltd.
10 Roybridge Gate, Unit 200
Vaughan, ON
Canada L4H 3M8
www.kertzer.com

Lion Brand Yarns
135 Kero Rd.
Carlstadt, NJ 07072
lionbrand.com

Knitting Fever Inc./Noro
PO Box 336
315 Bayview Ave.
Amityville, NY 11701
knittingfever.com

Tahki/Stacy Charles Inc.
70-30 80th St., Bldg. 36
Ridgewood, NY 11385
tahkistacycharles.com
in Canada: Diamond Yarn

Westminster Fibers/Rowan
165 Ledge St.
Nashua, NH 03060
www.westminsterfibers.com
in Canada: Diamond Yarn

INDEX

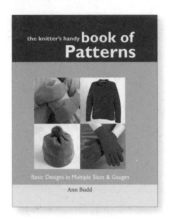